DISEASES & DISORDERS

Parasitic Diseases

Lizabeth Craig

LUCENT BOOKS
A part of Gale, Cengage Learning

GALE
CENGAGE Learning·

Farmington Hills, Mich • San Francisco • New York • Waterville, Maine
Meriden, Conn • Mason, Ohio • Chicago

LIBRARY OF CONGRESS CATALOGING-IN-PUBLICATION DATA

Craig, Lizabeth.
  Parasitic diseases / by Lizabeth Craig.
    pages cm. -- (Diseases and disorders)
  Summary: "This title in Lucent's Diseases and Disorders series focuses on parasitic diseases. It details what parasitic diseases are, as well as the various types (Protozoan, Helminth, Ectoparasites). The title discuss the causes and symptoms of each type of parasitic disease as well as prevention. It also explores research being done in a global effort to control or eradicate these diseases"-- Provided by publisher.
  Includes bibliographical references and index.
  ISBN 978-1-4205-1245-8 (hardback)
  1. Parasitic diseases--Juvenile literature. I. Title.
  RC119.C73 2015
  616.9'6--dc23
                                                         2015009102

Lucent Books
27500 Drake Rd.
Farmington Hills, MI 48331

ISBN-13: 978-1-4205-1245-8
ISBN-10: 1-4205-1245-5

Printed in the United States of America
1 2 3 4 5 6 7 19 18 17 16 15

Table of Contents

"The Most Difficult Puzzles Ever Devised"

Charles Best, one of the pioneers in the search for a cure for diabetes, once explained what it is about medical research that intrigued him so. "It's not just the gratification of knowing one is helping people," he confided, "although that probably is a more heroic and selfless motivation. Those feelings may enter in, but truly, what I find best is the feeling of going toe to toe with nature, of trying to solve the most difficult puzzles ever devised. The answers are there somewhere, those keys that will solve the puzzle and make the patient well. But how will those keys be found?"

Since the dawn of civilization, nothing has so puzzled people—and often frightened them, as well—as the onset of illness in a body or mind that had seemed healthy before. A seizure, the inability of a heart to pump, the sudden deterioration of muscle tone in a small child—being unable to reverse such conditions or even to understand why they occur was unspeakably frustrating to healers. Even before there were names for such conditions, even before they were understood at all, each was a reminder of how complex the human body was, and how vulnerable.

While our grappling with understanding diseases has been frustrating at times, it has also provided some of humankind's most heroic accomplishments. Alexander Fleming's accidental discovery in 1928 of a mold that could be turned into penicillin has resulted in the saving of untold millions of lives. The isolation of the enzyme insulin has reversed what was once a death sentence for anyone with diabetes. There have been great strides in combating conditions for which there is not yet a cure, too. Medicines can help AIDS patients live longer, diagnostic tools such as mammography and ultrasounds can help doctors find tumors while they are treatable, and laser surgery techniques have made the most intricate, minute operations routine.

This "toe-to-toe" competition with diseases and disorders is even more remarkable when seen in a historical continuum. An astonishing amount of progress has been made in a very short time. Just two hundred years ago, the existence of germs as a cause of some diseases was unknown. In fact, it was less than 150 years ago that a British surgeon named Joseph Lister had difficulty persuading his fellow doctors that washing their hands before delivering a baby might increase the chances of a healthy delivery (especially if they had just attended to a diseased patient)!

Each book in Lucent's Diseases and Disorders series explores a disease or disorder and the knowledge that has been accumulated (or discarded) by doctors through the years. Each book also examines the tools used for pinpointing a diagnosis, as well as the various means that are used to treat or cure a disease. Finally, new ideas are presented—techniques or medicines that may be on the horizon.

Frustration and disappointment are still part of medicine, for not every disease or condition can be cured or prevented. But the limitations of knowledge are being pushed outward constantly; the "most difficult puzzles ever devised" are finding challengers every day.

Unwelcome Guests

Throughout the natural world, plants and animals live together and rely on each other for food, protection, transportation, and reproduction. Many hundreds of relationships exist between organisms of different species. Cattle birds follow the cattle in the fields and gobble up the insects that are stirred up by their hooves. The birds get fed and the cattle are relieved of insect bites. Clown fish live among the stinging tentacles of sea anemones, getting protection from predators, while the anemones are protected from anemone-eating fish and nourished by the droppings of the clown fish.

Some relationships between organisms, however, are not mutually beneficial. In some relationships one member of the partnership benefits, but the other is actually harmed. This is a parasitic relationship. Parasites take what they need from their host, but in return they can cause sickness and even eventual death to the host. Almost every kind of plant and animal can be used for survival by some kind of parasite. Mistletoe, so popular at Christmas, lives in trees and deprives them of water and nutrients. Fleas and ticks feed on the blood animals such as dogs and cats and can make the animals sick. Some wasps lay their eggs on the body of an ant or a caterpillar, which is then used for food by the hatching wasp larvae. Fossilized remains suggest that even the dinosaurs had parasites living in and on them.

Human beings are no exception to this rule. Humans are hosts to hundreds of different parasitic organisms. Some live inside the human body, such as roundworms and flatworms;

others live on the outside, such as fleas, ticks, mites, and lice. Most are easily visible to the naked eye. Others are microscopic, such as the one-celled protozoan that causes the killer disease malaria. All use the human body as their own personal cafeteria, happily living in and on human organs and tissues, almost always at the expense of their human host.

People, Parasites, and Evolution

For as long as human beings have existed on the planet, parasites have kept them company. "Sometime, about 150,000 years ago," writes F.E.G. Cox, "*Homo sapiens* emerged in eastern Africa and spread throughout the world, possibly in several waves, until 15,000 years ago at the end of the Ice Age humans had migrated to and inhabited virtually the whole of the face of the Earth, bringing some parasites with them and collecting others on the way."[1] What is known about these ancient parasites comes from studying fossilized human feces, called coprolites. The earliest evidence of parasitic infection comes from the discovery of eggs from a parasitic worm called a lung fluke, found in coprolites from northern Chile that date to about 5900 B.C. Tapeworm eggs and even a fossilized worm have been found in Egyptian mummies as old as four thousand years.

About ten thousand years ago, humans learned to grow their own food crops and to domesticate animals such as chickens, cattle, and pigs. They stopped migrating, settled into communities, and built towns and cities. With more and more people living closely together, the spread of parasitic infections such as malaria increased rapidly. Humans also picked up new parasites, especially worms, from their livestock and passed them on to each other. The opening of trade routes between cities and countries helped spread parasitic infections to a much wider area. The expansion of the Roman Empire throughout Europe, the Middle East, and North Africa made malaria so widespread it was referred to as the "Roman fever." With the European discovery of the New World in the fifteenth century, the age of world exploration that followed it, and the development of the African slave trade, parasites accompanied humans around the globe.

Written Records

Almost as soon as humans began to record their lives with writing, they began to write about parasites. These ancient writings include descriptions of intestinal worms only; microscopic parasites would not be discovered until the invention of the microscope in the seventeenth century. The first known written records about what are probably parasitic infections come from ancient Egypt. The Ebers papyrus, discovered by German Egyptologist Georg Ebers in 1873, is dated to about 1500 B.C. Written in ancient Egyptian hieroglyphics, it describes more than seven hundred spells, formulas, and remedies for treating various disorders, including diseases that are almost certainly infections by parasitic worms. In ancient Greece Hippocrates (460 B.C.–370 B.C.), the "Father of Western Medicine," wrote extensively about parasitic worms in humans and other animals. In his work *On Airs, Waters, and Places*, he wrote a description of what may be a parasitic worm infection, because of the mention of stagnant water and swollen bellies: "If there be no rivers, but the inhabitants drink the waters of fountains, and such as are stagnant and marshy, they must necessarily have prominent bellies and enlarged spleens."[2] Other parasitic diseases are also well documented, but the writers at the time did not know that they were caused by parasites. Texts from other ancient cultures such as India and China also refer to what could be parasitic diseases such as hookworm and malaria, though these writers, too, could not have known the actual cause of these diseases without the benefit of a microscope.

In medieval times (roughly from the fifth to the fifteenth century), the Persian physician Avicenna (980–1037) wrote about parasitic worms in animals and in his human patients. Like the Greeks, Avicenna also wrote about parasitic diseases caused by microscopic organisms, although without the microscope, he could not have made the connection between the parasites and the diseases they caused. At this time in history, most physicians subscribed to the theory that illness was caused by "miasmas"—their word for "foul air."

The first microscopic parasite to be described was the single-celled organism giardia, observed by the inventor of the

The Persian physician Avicenna wrote about parasitic worms in
animals and humans in the eleventh century.

microscope, the Dutchman Anton van Leeuwenhoek, in 1681.
Not until the late nineteenth century, however, with the development of the germ theory, did it become possible to connect
specific organisms with their diseases. At this time the life
cycles of parasitic organisms were first described in accurate
detail, and their role in human disease was defined.

Parasitic Diseases Today

Today hundreds of different parasites cause human disease in all parts of the world. The burden is especially great in poorer tropical and subtropical countries, in which the climate is warm most of the time and where public health systems are inadequate to prevent and treat these diseases. Malaria is still the deadliest of parasitic diseases, killing approximately 660,000 people worldwide each year, most of whom are children in sub-Saharan Africa.

A group of seventeen diseases called neglected tropical diseases (NTDs) affect more than 1 billion people worldwide, mostly in outlying areas of developing countries. Eleven of the seventeen recognized NTDs are caused by parasites. These diseases represent not only a physical burden in terms of illness, but also an economic burden in terms of lost income, missed school days, and costs related to prevention and treatment. These illnesses are called "neglected" diseases because, despite the enormous toll they take in human suffering, relatively little attention has been paid to them in terms of publicity, research, and funding. Says science writer Carl Zimmer:

> Most of the past century's research on parasites has gone into trying to fight the ones that cause devastating illness in humans, such as malaria, AIDS, and tuberculosis. But otherwise, parasites have largely been neglected. Scientists have treated them with indifference, even contempt, viewing them as essentially hitchhikers on life's road. But recent research reveals that parasites are remarkably sophisticated and tenacious and may be as important to ecosystems as the predators at the top of the food chain.[3]

Undertreated parasitic diseases also occur in the United States. Neglected parasitic infections in the United States include five diseases that have been singled out by the Centers for Disease Control and Prevention (CDC) as needing more funding for research and treatment. These illnesses include Chagas' disease, cysticercosis (sis-ti-ser-KOH-sis), toxocariasis (toxo-car-I-asis), toxoplasmosis (toxo-plas-MO-sis), and trichomoniasis (trik-o-mo-NY-asis). According to the CDC, these five diseases cause illness in millions of Americans each year, mostly minorities, the poor, and immigrants from Central and South America. "Parasitic infections affect millions around the world causing seizures, blindness, infertility, heart failure, and even death," says CDC director Tom Frieden. "They're more common in the U.S. than people realize and yet there is so much that we don't know about them. We need research to learn more about these infections, and action to better prevent and treat them."[4]

Parasites and the diseases they cause have always been part of human existence and likely always will. New parasitic organisms and their effects on human health are still being discovered. For example, some parasitic worm species that usually affect wildlife are finding their way into the human population by infecting rats, which then share them with humans in areas where people and rats live together. The authors of a 2014 Australian study write, "We discovered 32% of parasites found in rats are also found in humans. With both rat and human populations on the rise, there is concern that urban sprawl and global spread of invasive species will expose formerly isolated wildlife and their parasites to people and vice versa."[5] The field of parasitology continues to grow as new illnesses are discovered and new ways to control and treat older ones are developed.

CHAPTER ONE

What Are Parasites?

"**E**very living thing has at least one parasite that lives inside it or on it," says science writer Carl Zimmer.

Many, like leopard frogs and humans, have many more. There's a parrot in Mexico with thirty different species of mites on its feathers alone. And the parasites themselves have parasites, and some of those parasites have parasites of their own. . . . Scientists have no idea just how many species of parasites there are, but they do know one dazzling thing: parasites make up the majority of species on Earth. According to one estimate, parasites may outnumber free-living species four to one. In other words, the study of life is, for the most part, parasitology.[6]

A parasite is any organism, plant or animal, which gets all of its survival needs met by taking what it needs from another living organism. The organism on which a parasite lives is called its host. In this kind of relationship, the host suffers in some way because of the parasite; the parasite does not give anything back to its host, nor does it benefit the host in any way. Parasitism is unique among relationships in the natural world because instead of living out in the environment, a parasite must spend all or part of its life in or on a host organism. From the website About Bioscience: "Parasitism comprises an ecological relationship between two individuals of different species where the parasite's environment is another living organism. Unlike the environment of free-living plants and animals, the environment of the parasite can fight back. Parasites and hosts are locked into a continuous struggle for survival."[7]

Parasitism is one of several types of relationships, called symbiotic relationships, in which different species interact and live with one another. Parasitism is by far the most common symbiotic relationship; it is estimated that there are more different species of parasitic organisms than all nonparasitic organisms combined. More than 50 percent of all animal organisms on the Earth are parasites, and almost all species that are not parasites themselves, including human beings, serve as host to one or more kinds of parasites. Human beings in every part of the world serve as hosts to several hundred different species of parasitic organisms.

The parasitic head louse attaches itself to its host's hair.

Naming Organisms

In the eighteenth century Swedish biologist Carl Linnaeus created a way of naming all living organisms in a scientific way so that scientists of all countries and all languages could understand each other when they spoke of particular organisms. His system classified all organisms into groups based on common characteristics. The largest groups are the kingdoms. There are five kingdoms: Monera (bacteria), Protista (protozoans and algae), Fungi (fungi, mosses, yeasts, and mushrooms), Plantae (plants), and Animalia (animals). The smaller groups after kingdom are (in order of size) phylum, class, order, family, genus, and species. As the groups get smaller, the organisms in them have more and more in common.

All organisms can be called by a two-word scientific name, made up of their genus name and species name. In scientific writing the name is written in italics. The first name is capitalized, and the second name is not. The names are usually Latin or Greek. For example, the common house cat is *Felis catus.* The domestic dog is named *Canis familiaris.* The name may be a version of the person who discovered it; for example, the bacteria that causes bubonic plague is named *Yersinia pestis,* after Alexandre Yersin. Human beings are named *Homo sapiens.* Modern humans are the only species left of the genus *Homo* (which means "human" in Latin).

Parasites have scientific names, too. Scientists everywhere know that when one of them says *Plasmodium falciparum,* he or she is talking about one of the parasites that cause malaria. The guinea worm is *Dracunculus medinensis. Ixodes scapularis* is the deer tick that spreads Lyme disease, and *Pulex irritans* is the human flea.

Symbiotic Relationships

A symbiotic relationship is one in which two or more species live together and interact in some way. The word *symbiotic* means "life living together." The word was originally used to describe people living together in close-knit communities, but in 1877 German biologist Albert Bernhard Frank used the word to refer to relationships between other living things. Two years later the German biologist Heinrich Anton de Bary refined it to mean organisms of different species living together.

In the natural world symbiotic relationships occur between animals, plants, microbes, fungi, or any combination of these. Some symbiotic relationships are beneficial to both partners in the relationship. Some are beneficial to only one, but the other is neither helped nor harmed. In others one partner benefits while the other partner is actually harmed or even killed. In all cases the partners in the relationship share close physical contact in a long-term, possibly lifelong, relationship. There are three major kinds of symbiotic relationship, defined by how each partner in the relationship is affected by the other. They are called mutualism, commensalism, and parasitism.

These ants protect aphids from predators in return for a sweet liquid secreted by the aphids, in an example of a mutually symbiotic relationship.

Mutualism

Mutualism is a symbiotic relationship in which both partners benefit from the relationship. Sometimes the benefit is in the form of food or nutrients, and sometimes the benefit is in the form of a service such as protection, transportation, or spreading seeds. In some mutualistic relationships both partners are completely dependent on each other in order to survive; without one, the other would die. This is called obligate mutualism. A classic example of an obligate symbiotic relationship is the relationship between flowering plants and honeybees. The bees get the food they need from the plants, and the plants rely on the bees to disseminate pollen so that the plants can reproduce. Neither of these organisms would be able to survive and reproduce without the other.

In other symbiotic relationships the interaction is helpful to each partner but not absolutely necessary for survival. This is called facultative mutualism. An example is the relationship between the oxpecker bird and the cattle it follows. The birds ride on the backs of the cattle and eat the insects that land on them, and the cattle are relieved of the insect pests. Both animals benefit, but neither is entirely reliant on the other for survival.

Commensalism

Commensalism is a relationship between organisms in which one partner benefits but the other is not really affected either way. A familiar example is the relationship between the remora fish and the shark. The remora benefits by attaching itself to the shark for transportation and by feeding on food that falls from the shark's mouth. The shark, however, is neither helped by this nor harmed by it. Some commensalistic relationships last for many years; others last only a short time.

There are several kinds of commensalism. Phoresy (FOR-a-see) is when one animal attaches itself to another only for transportation; for example, mites that "hitch a ride" on the backs of flies or beetles. Inquilinism (in-KWIL-in-ism) is one organism using the other for shelter, such as birds living in holes in trees. Metabiosis (meta-bi-OH-sis) means that one organism

Parasitology

Parasitology is the study of parasites, their hosts, and the relationships between them. People who are interested in a career in parasitology have many options to choose from to specialize in certain areas of parasitology.

Medical parasitology specializes in parasitic diseases and conditions of human beings. Parasitologists work with many other health- and science-related disciplines such as biology, ecology, epidemiology, chemistry, genetics, and public health. They work to learn more about parasite biology, the diseases caused by parasites, the insects that spread the diseases, medicines to treat and cure the diseases, and ways to prevent the diseases. Veterinary parasitologists do much the same kind of work, but they focus on parasitic diseases of animals, especially pets and livestock animals. They also work with medical parasitologists on those diseases that can be spread from animals to people. Other parasitologists study plant parasites for the agricultural industry, not only those that affect plants directly, but also those that can be used as biological control for insects that destroy crops. Parasitologists also work with wildlife managers to help control parasites in animals in the wild, including mammals, birds, and fish and other aquatic animals. There are many other specialized areas of study in parasitolgy.

Education for becoming a parasitologist starts with a broad range of basic study in biology and chemistry beginning in high school. Knowledge and training in computer science, mathematics, writing, and public speaking is also important. Most fields in parasitology require at least a bachelor of science degree in college, often followed by a graduate degree such as a master's or PhD. Many parasitologists are doctors who have graduated from medical school.

uses the remains of another for food or shelter, such the hermit crab living in a seashell or vultures feeding on a dead animal.

Parasitism

In a parasitic relationship the parasitic organism benefits in some way, but the host is harmed and in some cases even killed by the parasite. There are several different forms that a parasitic relationship might take. For example, some parasites are necrotrophic, which means that they produce toxins that kill part of their host plant and get nutrients from the host's dead cells. Others, called biotrophic parasites, need their host's cells to be alive in order to survive and so do not produce toxins. Obligate parasites are completely dependent on a host for survival, and facultative parasites can live without a host if they have to.

Some parasites, such as fleas, are temporary visitors and spend only a short time with their host. Others, such as the organism that causes malaria, spend part of their life cycle with one host and another part with another host. Still others, such as the amoeba that causes dysentery, spend part of their lives in the environment and the rest in a host. Endoparasites live inside their host's body, either in a body cavity or actually inside the host's cells and tissues. Ectoparasites live out on the surface of their host. Parasites that affect animals and people are grouped into three main categories—protozoans, helminths, and arthropods.

Protozoans

Protozoans are single-celled, microscopic parasites. There are more than one hundred thousand different species of protozoans. They live primarily in the gut, the bloodstream, or the tissues of their hosts. Protozoans are further classified into four groups according to their structure and how they move— amoebas, flagellates, ciliates, and sporozoans.

Amoebas are simple, blob-like protozoans that move by crawling over surfaces, constantly changing their shape as they move. Flagellates have a long, tail-like structure called a flagellum (plural: flagella), which they use for moving through

Parasites on Parasites

Humans and other animals are not the only ones that must deal with parasites. Some parasites can also get parasites of their own. These "parasites of parasites" are called hyperparasites. For example, a tiny gnat-like insect called a *Culicoides* midge has been seen using mosquitoes as a host, feeding on the blood that the mosquito has just taken from its own host. The midge has also been observed feeding on the body of the blister beetle, which is parasitic during its larval stage. The cabbage butterfly caterpillar can be parasitized by the larvae of two different kinds of wasps, both of which can be parasitized by the larvae of a third kind of wasp.

Hyperparasites can even have parasites themselves, and the parasite-host chain can get quite complicated. For example, a parasitic blowfly uses young birds in their nests as hosts for their blood-sucking larvae. When the larvae fall off the bird, a parasitic wasp feeds on them, at the same time transmitting a parasitic bacterium called *Wolbachia* to the larvae. Even the bacterium is vulnerable to a microscopic parasitic virus called a bacteriophage.

Parasitic wasp larvae attached to a caterpillar illustrate the behavior of hyperparasites.

water or body fluids by whipping it back and forth. Ciliates are surrounded by tiny, hair-like projections called cilia, which move back and forth in waves and propel the ciliate in any direction. Sporozoans, unlike other protozoans, have no movement structures at all and cannot move by themselves, but rely on other animals to carry them from host to host.

Helminths

Helminths are worms. The word *helminth* refers to all worms, but not all helminths are parasites (the common earthworm is a helminth, but not a parasite). There are more than fifty thousand species of parasitic helminths that infect people as well as almost all other vertebrates (animals with a backbone). They are multicellular, much larger than protozoans, and very easily visible to the naked eye.

Colorized scanning electron micrograph of a dog roundworm (Toxocara canis). In this image, showing the front of the worm, the worm's mouth with three serrated "lips" is clearly visible. This species ranges in size from 1.5–4 inches (4–10 cm); females are larger. The adult animals live in the small intestines of infected dogs.

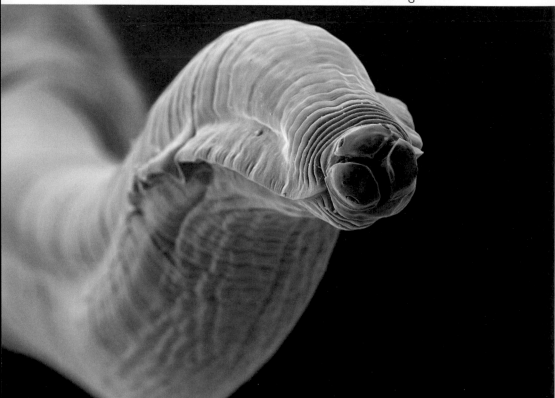

Helminths may be flat or round and tubular. Roundworms are called nematodes (NEE-ma-todes). They have a mouth at their front end, a long digestive tract, and an inner, fluid-filled body cavity that helps keep their bodies firm. They have muscles that they use to move themselves forward or to thrash back and forth when they are touched.

Flatworms, or platyhelminths (plat-ee-HEL-minths), do not have internal body cavities, although they do have a primitive mouth that leads into a small digestive pouch. They can also take in oxygen and nutrients through their bodies. The species of flatworms that affect humans the most are divided into two groups—the cestodes, or tapeworms, and trematodes, or flukes. Tapeworms have long bodies made up of many small segments, with a special organ at the front end called a scolex, which they use to hold on to the inside of their host's intestinal tract. Flukes have leaf-shaped bodies with two suckers at the front end. Depending on the species, they may attach themselves in the liver, lung, pancreas, intestine, or bloodstream of their host.

Arthropods

Arthropods are the class of animals that includes crustaceans (crabs, lobsters, shrimp), arachnids (spiders, scorpions, ticks), and insects. Arthropods have jointed legs (*arthro* means "joint" and *pod* means "leg" or "foot.") They have segmented bodies made of two or three segments, and most have visible heads. Their bodies are covered by a hard outer layer called an exoskeleton, which they shed periodically as they grow larger. Parasitic arthropods are ectoparasites, living on the outside of their host's body. Most are either insects or arachnids.

Most parasitic insects belong to one of three main groups—fleas, flies and mosquitoes, and lice. There are about twenty-five hundred different species of flea. Fleas move from host to host using limbs especially designed for jumping. Mammals are their favorite host animals, but some live on birds. Fleas feed on the blood of their host, and many can transmit disease to their host through their bite. A well-known example of a flea-borne disease is bubonic plague.

An electron micrograph of the common cat flea, an arthropod.
There are about twenty-five hundred different species of flea.

Flies and mosquitoes include well over 120,000 species. They generally spend very little time on their host—just long enough to get a meal of their host's blood. Flies and mosquitoes can transmit disease-causing organisms to their host when they feed, such as African sleeping sickness and malaria.

Lice are parasitic during all stages of their life cycle. Lice live mainly in hair-covered areas of the body such as the scalp, pubic area, or even in beards and eyebrows. They spend their entire life cycle on their host, feeding on the host's blood. They are easily spread from person to person but rarely cause disease in people.

Parasitic arachnids include ticks and mites. Ticks can cause illness by themselves, such as anemia and tick paralysis, or they can spread other disease-causing organisms to their hosts, such as Lyme disease and Rocky Mountain spotted fever. Mites are microscopic arachnids and include more than forty thousand species. They may use mammals, birds, reptiles, crustaceans, insects, or fish as hosts. Mites cause mange in dogs and skin diseases such as scabies in humans. Chiggers are a kind of mite that causes an intensely itchy rash. Dust mites can cause reactions such as asthma or dermatitis.

Transmission of Parasites

There are many ways in which a parasite can get into or onto its host's body. The method of transmission of a particular parasite depends on the part of the body on which the parasite lives. The most common transmission methods for parasites include through food or water, from the bite of nonparasitic arthropods such as mosquitoes, from other animals such as cows or pigs, and by direct contact with the parasite itself.

In underdeveloped parts of the world, sanitation practices and water-treatment methods are often inadequate to provide the people living there with clean water and food. Contaminated water is a serious problem in many parts of the world and causes millions of illnesses and deaths each year. Many kinds of protozoans, amoebas, or helminths that live in the digestive tract are spread by drinking water that has been contaminated with fecal waste from other infected people or animals. Common waterborne parasitic diseases include guinea worm, amoebic dysentery, giardiasis, and schistosomiasis. Waterborne intestinal parasites can also be spread in more developed parts of the world, such as the United States, by recreational activities like swimming if contaminated water from pools, lakes, rivers, or the ocean is swallowed. The most common illness that is picked up in this way is diarrhea caused by protozoans.

Protozoans such as giardias (gee-AR-de-a) and cryptosporidiums (cripto-spor-ID-ium), and helminths such as roundworms and tapeworms, can also be spread through food that is contaminated with the parasite or its eggs. Usually the food has been undercooked or has been cooked in unsanitary conditions by people with poor hygiene. These infections may also be caused if fruits and vegetables that have been contaminated with human or animal feces in the soil are not washed or are washed with contaminated water.

Parasites transmitted by food or water cause a variety of symptoms, depending on the particular organism. The most common include diarrhea and abdominal pain, but parasitic helminths can also cause skin sores, malnutrition, muscular pain, brain disorders, and many other symptoms.

Arthropods

Parasitic insects and arthropods that carry and transmit disease-causing organisms (called pathogens) in their bodies are called disease vectors, and the diseases they carry are called vector-borne diseases. For example, the bacterium that causes plague is carried in the gut of a flea. The flea is the vector, and it transmits the plague bacterium to its host when it bites the host. Many parasitic protozoans are carried by insect vectors. The insect vector for malaria is the anopheles (a-NOF-a-leez) mosquito. For sleeping sickness, the insect vector is the tsetse fly.

Most parasitic organisms transmitted through insect vectors spend a portion of their life cycle circulating through the bloodstream of their host. From the bloodstream, they can travel to and damage other organs. For example, the parasite that causes Chagas' disease is carried by the so-called kissing bug and can damage the heart and digestive tract. Leishmania parasites, which are carried by sand flies and cause the disease leishmaniasis (leesh-man-EYE-asis), can infect the skin and cause sores and may also affect the spleen, liver, and bone marrow.

Animal Transmission of Parasites

A disease that is spread from animals to people is called a zoonotic (zoh-o-notic) disease, or zoonosis. Influenza is an example of a zoonotic disease because some strains of the influenza virus can be picked up from pigs (swine flu) or fowl (bird flu). Many parasitic diseases can be considered zoonotic because other animals are the source of the parasite.

There are several ways in which a zoonotic parasite might be transmitted to people. If a cow or pig is infected with a parasite, people who eat the meat of that animal, especially if it is raw or undercooked, may pick up the parasite. An example of this is trichinosis, a roundworm carried by domestic pigs as well as wild hogs, bears, and other mammals. (Due to strict food regulations, trichinosis from domestic pigs is now very rare in the United States.) Animal parasites can also be transmitted to people if food or water is contaminated with feces from infected animals.

Some parasites can come from household pets. Fleas and ticks are very commonly spread from pets to people. Dogs and cats, especially puppies and kittens, can be infected with roundworm or hookworm. People can pick up the eggs of these worms by handling the pet's feces and not washing their hands before they eat, and children may pick them up from playing outside where the pet has passed feces. Toxoplasmosis is a parasitic disease that completes its life cycle in cats. It is

Fleas and ticks are commonly spread by dogs and cats to people.

excreted in the cat's feces and can be transmitted to people in this way. Although cats rarely have symptoms of toxoplasmosis, it can be a serious disease in people because it can be passed to an unborn baby and cause problems with development in the womb.

Other ways in which people can get parasites include direct skin penetration. For example, the intestinal nematode called hookworm can enter the body by burrowing through the soles of the feet. Some parasitic organisms can spread through sexual contact, such as trichomoniasis (a vaginal infection, not to be confused with trichinosis) and pubic lice (commonly called "crabs").

Diagnosing Parasitic Diseases

Diagnosing a parasitic disease can be difficult because of the sheer number of different species of parasite that can infect people. In addition, many kinds of parasite can live in the body for years without causing symptoms. Helminths and ectoparasites are relatively easy to diagnose because they are more easily seen with the naked eye. Protozoan illnesses, however, can be more difficult to pin down.

The first step in diagnosis is for the patient to give a complete health history. The doctor or other health-care worker will ask the patient to give a detailed account of his or her symptoms— what they are, when they started, if they are constant or come and go, if anything in particular is helpful in relieving them, and so forth. The doctor will ask about other health conditions that may account for the symptoms. If the doctor suspects a parasitic disease, he or she may ask about the patient's travel history to see whether the patient has been to a country where parasitic diseases are common. The doctor will then perform a thorough physical examination of the patient to look for signs of other diseases and for visible parasites. If no parasites are visible, laboratory tests will be ordered to help arrive at a diagnosis. The specific tests chosen will depend on the information given during the initial examination.

A fecal ova and parasite test looks for intestinal parasites and their eggs (ova) in a fecal sample. The sample is taken to the laboratory, where a thin smear of the sample is examined under a microscope. A portion of it may be treated with special stains that add color to the parasites to make the organisms more visible. The test is repeated for at least three days in a row in order to confirm the result.

A variety of blood tests can be done that detect the presence of parasites in the blood. Blood serology is done to look for parasite antigens or antibodies in the blood. Antigens are substances on the surface of a disease-causing organism that are recognized by the body as foreign. Antigens trigger the body's immune response to fight the invading organism. Antibodies, which are special proteins made by the body in response to the antigen, destroy the organism. If antigens are the "enemy," antibodies are the "soldiers." Serology tests can detect the presence of antigens or the antibodies made in response to the antigens.

Another kind of blood test is a blood smear. A smear involves spreading a very thin layer of blood on a glass slide. The sample is stained and examined under a microscope to look for the presence of microscopic parasites such as the protozoan that causes malaria. Once the diagnosis of a parasitic disease is made, treatment can begin. Treatment will depend entirely on what kind of parasite it is and on what treatment methods are available in the part of the world in which the patient lives.

CHAPTER TWO

Protozoans

Protozoans were among the earliest life-forms to appear on the planet. The name *protozoan* comes from *proto*, which means "first," and *zoa*, which means "animals." Protozoans are not actually classified as animals, however, nor are they classified as plants or fungi. They are part of a group called protists. Some protists are animal-like, such as protozoans; other protists are more plant-like, such as algae and seaweed.

Protozoans are the most numerous of all organisms. In fact, there are more protozoans on the earth than any other kind of animal or plant. They are a very diverse group of organisms; it is estimated that more than fifty thousand different kinds of protozoan currently exist, with another thirty-four thousand known from fossil records to have existed in the past. Most protozoans are not parasitic but are free-living in water or soil. Protozoan organisms can be found in every part of the Earth, from the tops of mountains to rivers and streams to the bottom of the ocean.

Protozoans are by far the smallest in size of the three groups of parasites; most of them are microscopic in size, but still larger than bacteria. Because of their very small size, their existence was not discovered until after the invention of the microscope in the late 1600s. Even then, their connection with disease was not fully understood until the late 1800s, when the germ theory of disease, which connected specific organisms with specific diseases, was developed by Louis Pasteur and others.

All protozoans are single-celled organisms. They are eukaryotic, which means they have a nucleus that is surrounded by a membrane and contains their genetic material. Their bodies are encased in a cell membrane, and some have an additional outer surface layer called a pellicle, which is rigid enough to allow the organism to maintain a more or less fixed shape. Depending on their type, they have a variety of other internal structures within their bodies called organelles, which have various functions and allow them to live and behave much like animals. For example, they can move around using various methods of movement. They cannot make their own food like plants do but must take in and digest food particles from their environment, including bacteria, algae, or even other protozoans. Some eat by surrounding and absorbing their food. Others have a cytosome, or cell mouth, which they use for taking in food. They also reproduce themselves. Some reproduce asexually by simply dividing their bodies in two. This is the most common form of protozoan reproduction. Others go through a complex series of sexual reproductive stages that include male and female forms.

Types of Protozoan

There are four main groups of protozoan organisms, described by the ways in which they move: amoebas, flagellates, ciliates, and sporozoans. Amoebas (a-MEE-bas) are the simplest of the protozoans. They look like little blobs of clear material, called cytoplasm. They move by slowly crawling over surfaces, constantly changing their shape as they move. They do this by extending forward one or more portions of their cell membrane, into which the rest of their cytoplasm flows. These temporary extensions of their bodies are called pseudopods, or false feet. This is also how they surround their food, absorb it into their bodies, and digest it. (Human white blood cells also use this kind of movement to surround invading organisms and destroy them.) There are approximately 11,550 species of amoeba. Although several of these can cause disease in humans, only one of them, called *Entamoeba histolytica*, is considered a parasite. It causes an intestinal illness called amoebic dysentery and can also cause abscesses in the liver.

Flagellates (FLA-jel-ates) have bodies that may be round, oval, or long and thin. They have a long, tail-like structure called a flagellum, which they move back and forth like a whip in order to move themselves around. (The human sperm cell, while not a protozoan, is an example of a flagellated cell.) Some flagellates have soft cell membranes and can be seen to change their shape as they move, similarly to amoebas. Others have more rigid bodies and are able to propel themselves forward without even using their flagellum. Of the approximately sixty-nine hundred species of flagellate, about eighteen hundred are parasitic to animals or humans. The most common diseases caused by flagellates include giardiasis, leishmaniasis, African sleeping sickness, and Chagas' disease.

Ciliate (SIL-ee-ate) bodies are surrounded on all sides by many tiny hair-like projections called cilia. The cilia move rap-

This illustration shows the basic parts that make up a protozoan.

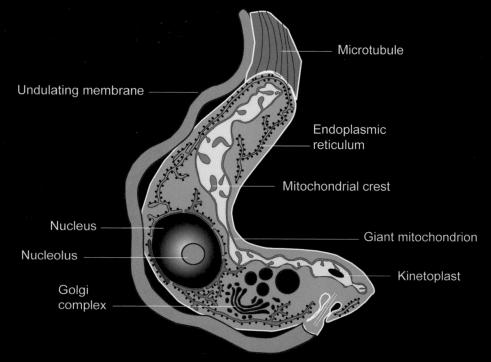

Microtubule

Undulating membrane

Endoplasmic reticulum

Mitochondrial crest

Nucleus

Giant mitochondrion

Nucleolus

Kinetoplast

Golgi complex

Trypanosoma congolense

idly back and forth in an organized, wave-like fashion to move the ciliate in any direction. About twenty-five hundred of the known seventy-two hundred ciliate species are parasitic, but only one, called *Balantidium coli*, causes disease in humans—an intestinal illness called balantidiasis. Its normal host is the pig, in which it lives without causing illness. It is transmitted to people through food and water that have been contaminated with pig feces. Balantidiasis is not common, but it occurs more frequently in malnourished people who live in poor areas in close proximity to pigs. It causes severe diarrhea and can cause perforation of the large intestine, a very serious problem.

Sporozoans (spor-o-ZO-ans) are unlike other protozoans in that none of the more than fifty-six hundred known species are free-living; they are all parasitic to some other organism. Sporozoans are also unlike other protozoans in that they cannot move on their own and must rely on other animals to pass them on to new hosts. Sporozoan parasites cause diseases such as malaria, toxoplasmosis, and babesiosis. Some sporozoans, such as the ones that cause malaria and babesiosis, rely on more than one host during their life cycle and spend all stages of their life in a host animal. Others, such as toxoplasmosis, spend part of their life out in the environment, waiting to be picked up by a host animal.

Life Cycles of Protozoan Parasites

Depending on the species, the life cycles of protozoans can be simple, with just one stage, or they can be rather complex, with several stages. The term *trophozoite* refers to the stage of life during which the protozoan is actively feeding and multiplying; this is the stage during which it causes the most disease in people. Some species, such as trichomonas, cannot survive outside a host and spend their entire life in the trophozoite stage, passing directly from host to host through close physical contact. Most protozoans, however, have one or more additional stages in their lives.

The cyst stage is the stage during which a parasite is passed from its host's body and lives out in the environment, in the water or the soil. At this stage, it develops a protective membrane, or thickened cell wall, called a cyst, which helps it survive until it is picked up by a new host. A parasite in the cyst stage can survive outside a host for as much as a year or more, without the need for water or nutrients. Also during the cyst stage, the parasite multiplies itself inside the cyst. Once inside a new host's body, the cyst opens and releases new trophozoites. This life cycle is common among amoebas and the flagellates.

Some protozoan species, such as the sporozoan that causes malaria, have a third stage in their life cycle. Rather than pass directly from host to host or form cysts, they spend part of their life in the body of an intermediate host, called a vector. The vector is often an insect such as a mosquito or fly. When the insect feeds on an infected host, parasites are taken up by the insect and live there for a while. During this time in the insect, they grow and multiply rapidly, passing through several stages. Eventually, the parasites make their way into the insect's saliva. When the infected insect feeds on a new host, the parasites are injected through the insect's saliva into the new host, where they continue to grow, multiply, and cause illness.

Diseases Caused by Protozoans

Virtually all human beings carry one or more species of protozoans in or on their body at some time during their life, but not all protozoan species are parasitic. Some, such as some species of amoebas, live in the human body without causing any disease. Protozoan parasites are those species of protozoan that have adapted to the human body in ways that allow them to use its cells and tissues for survival. Most human protozoan diseases are caused by amoebas, flagellates, and sporozoans.

Protozoan diseases range from mild to life threatening. How severe the disease is depends largely on the number of parasites in the body and on the strength of the person's immune system to fight off the parasite. For example, a protozoan called *Pneumocystis carinii*, once thought to be a protozoan but now reclassifed as a fungus, may cause no illness in healthy people but can cause a severe, even fatal, form of pneumonia

Amoebas That Bite

Most parasitic amoebas, such as *Entamoeba histolytica*, the parasite that causes amoebic dysentery, devour their food (usually the tissue cells of their host) by surrounding it and absorbing it. A new study, however, published in April 2014 found that *E. histolytica* only eats cells this way if the cells are already dead. The study team, led by Katherine S. Ralston and William A. Petri of the University of Virginia, used advanced microscopes to observe the parasite. They used special dyes to stain the cell membranes of living human intestinal cells, then watched as the amoebas interacted with them. They observed that, rather than surround and absorb living cells, the amoebas actually "bite off" chunks of the cell membrane and engulf the bites until the cell finally disintegrates and dies, a process called trogocytosis. The amoebas then move on to a different living cell. In this way the parasites nibble their way through the intestinal wall until they burst out the other side and go on to infect other tissues and organs such as the blood or the liver. This behavior also was seen using human blood cells and immune cells.

This was the first time that an organism had been observed killing a cell by biting off pieces of it. The study team also found that they could block this process with drugs that prevent trogocytosis.

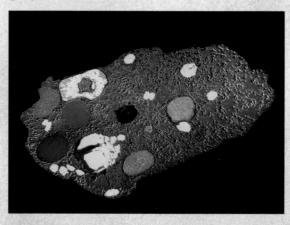

The *Entamoeba histolytica* causes an intestinal illness called amoebic dysentery and can also cause abscesses in the liver.

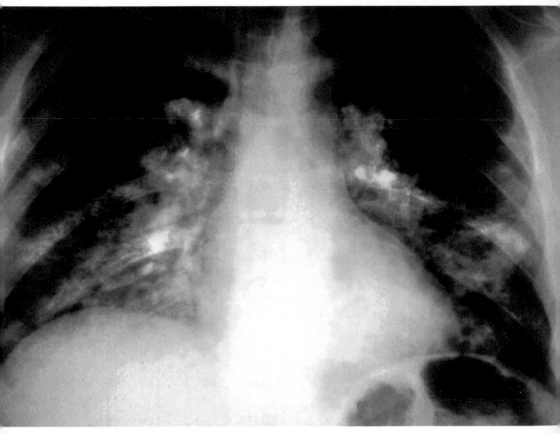

A chest X-ray shows a fungal infection of the lungs, in green, caused by *Pneumocystis carinii*.

in AIDS patients because of their weakened immune system. Other protozoan parasites, such as *Toxoplasma gondii*, were uncommon before the appearance of AIDS but have since become more widespread. Healthy people may carry a protozoan parasite in their body without getting sick, but they can still transmit the parasite to others.

Amoebic Dysentery

Amoebic dysentery (also called intestinal amoebiasis) is an intestinal illness caused by the amoeba *Entamoeba histolytica*. It is transmitted through food or water contaminated with the cysts of the parasite. Amoebic dysentery is most common in underdeveloped areas of the world in which sanitation methods are less than adequate and clean food and water are less common. It is not the same as "traveler's diarrhea," which is more often a bacterial illness.

Inside the human body, the trophozoites of the parasite invade the intestinal wall and can cause symptoms such as severe diarrhea, which may be bloody; abdominal pain; inflammation of the large intestine; weight loss; and anemia from blood loss. Left untreated, the infection can cause perforation, or a hole, in the intestine, which can set up a very dangerous and life-threatening inflammation of the entire abdominal cavity called peritonitis. The parasite can also travel through the bloodstream to the liver, where it can cause abscesses, pain in the upper abdomen, fever, chills, jaundice (a yellowish discoloration of the skin and eyes), and enlargement of the liver. Rarely, it can infect the lungs or the brain.

Amoebic dysentery is usually diagnosed by observation of the symptoms and confirmed by the presence of the amoeba in the stool. It is treated with fluid replacement, an antibiotic called metronidazole (Flagyl), and a medicine specific for the parasite called iodoquinol. Once treatment has begun, the illness lasts about two weeks. It can be avoided, however, by thorough hand washing and by eating and drinking only clean food and water.

Giardiasis

Giardiasis (gee-ar-DYE-asis) is caused by a flagellate called *Giardia lamblia*. It is the most common parasitic illness in humans worldwide. In 2013 an estimated 280 million people became infected with giardia. Infections occur in developed as well as underdeveloped countries. In developed countries such as the United States, it can be found in about 2 percent to 5 percent of the population. Giardiasis is also known to affect other mammals such as beavers, sheep, and cattle. It is considered a zoonotic illness because it can be spread from these and other animals to people.

Like amoebic dysentery, giardiasis is spread through water and food contaminated with cysts. It can also be spread directly from person to person through poor hygiene and improper hand washing. Once inside the body, it invades the cells of the small intestine and causes symptoms very similar to amoebic dysentery. Sometimes, people may be infected but show no symptoms. They can still spread the cysts to others, however. Giardiasis is most commonly diagnosed through symptoms and several tests that can detect evidence of the parasite in the stool. It is treated with fluids and antibiotics. It can be prevented by washing fruits and vegetables, boiling drinking or cooking water for ten minutes to kill the cysts, and thorough hand washing.

Trypanosomiasis

Trypanosomes (trip-AN-o-somes) are a large group of flagellate protozoans that cause a number of important vector-borne illnesses worldwide, including African sleeping sickness, Chagas' disease, and leishmaniasis. These are vector-borne diseases that complete part of their life cycle in the body of the insect vector.

African trypanosomiasis (trip-an-o-som-EYE-asis) is commonly called African sleeping sickness. It is caused by an organism called *Trypanosoma brucei* and is transmitted between its human and animal hosts by the tsetse fly. It also can be spread through blood transfusions, by sexual contact, and from a mother to an unborn baby across the placenta. It is most commonly seen in sub-Saharan Africa (African countries below the Sahara Desert) and is thought to affect approximately 60 million people worldwide at any given time.

Sleeping sickness has two stages of symptoms. In the first stage, symptoms begin with fever, headaches, and joint pains. When the parasites enter the lymphatic system (a part of the circulatory system involved in the body's infection control), the lymph nodes in the armpits, neck, or groin area may swell. Winterbottom's sign is a characteristic sign of sleeping sickness that appears as swollen lymph nodes on the back of the neck. The patient may also develop anemia or heart and kidney problems. In this first stage, treatment with various medications can cure the disease.

The second stage begins when the parasite passes into the brain through the bloodstream, and this stage is where the disease gets its name. Symptoms in this stage include confusion, reduced coordination, and disturbances in the sleep cycle, with periods of almost uncontrollable daytime sleepiness and nighttime insomnia. There is medical treatment for the disease at this stage, but even with treatment, the damage caused to the nervous system can be irreversible. Without treatment, progressive mental deterioration occurs, leading to coma and death.

This teenage girl's leg has a painful nodule that shows the initial bite site of a tsetse fly that transmitted the parasite *Trypanosoma brucei* into her body, causing sleeping sickness.

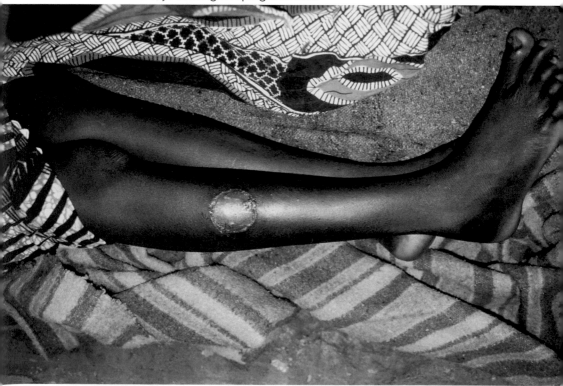

Chagas' Disease

Another important illness caused by a trypanosome is Chagas' disease, caused by *Trypanosoma cruzi*. It is most often spread by an insect vector commonly called "kissing bugs," which are native to Mexico, Central America, and South America. The disease, also called American trypanosomiasis, is fairly common in these areas, with about 8 million people currently affected. Recently, however, it has become more common in the United States. The CDC estimates that as many as three hundred thousand people in the United States may have it, and the CDC has listed Chagas' disease as a neglected parasitic infection, which means it is in need of more public health attention.

The Chagas' disease parasite is picked up by the kissing bug when it bites an infected animal or person. Because the bugs normally come out at night, they commonly bite on the face while the person is sleeping, which gives the insect its nickname. The parasite is spread when the infected insect deposits the parasite in its feces onto the skin of the host. It gets into the host either through the bite wound or through the eyes, nose, or mouth. This disease also has two phases of symptoms—an acute, or early, stage and a chronic, long-term stage. In the acute stage, symptoms can be mild and may include fever, fatigue, body aches, headache, rash, loss of appetite, diarrhea, and vomiting. The most recognizable symptom of acute Chagas' disease is Romaña's sign, which is a swelling of the eyelid on the side of the face near the bite wound, especially if the bug's feces were accidentally rubbed into the eye.

After several weeks, the disease enters the chronic stage. Many people never get symptoms in this stage and may not even know they have the disease. About 20 percent to 30 percent of people, however, develop serious problems in their heart, nervous system, or digestive system. The disease causes cell death in these systems and if untreated often leads to death from organ failure.

Leishmaniasis

In January 2003 seventy-two-year-old Alfred Eliah noticed a group of swollen bumps under his chin. Over the next month,

Chagas' Disease and Dogs

The so-called kissing bug, which is responsible for carrying the parasitic protozoan that causes Chagas' disease, normally lives in Mexico, Central America, and South America. Recently, however, the insect has been observed in states in the lower half of the United States as well. A study published in July 2014 showed an increased incidence of Chagas' disease in dogs in Texas. They get the disease either by being bitten by a kissing bug, eating another animal that is infected, or eating the feces of an infected animal.

As in people, dogs may show two stages of the disease. In the acute phase, usually seen in younger dogs, the dog may have symptoms such as diarrhea, fatigue, trouble walking, seizures, swollen lymph nodes, and even heart failure. In the chronic phase, usually in older dogs, the symptoms appear after a period of months to years with no symptoms at all.

Although dogs cannot pass the disease directly to humans, people are a target for the parasite, which can be transmitted to a person through an infected dog's bite. As people move around the United States, taking their dogs with them, the disease may be introduced into other parts of the country. Chagas' disease in dogs cannot be cured, so most veterinarians recommend that dogs with the infection be put down to prevent spread to humans.

the bumps grew and began to ooze a yellowish fluid. Eliah had recently returned from a trip to Peru, a country in western South America, and he remembered that a guide had a similar set of bumps on his arm, which he said were caused by a parasitic disease called leishmaniasis. Eliah went to the hospital, where his doctor consulted infectious disease specialist Pamela Nagami. "I had never seen a case of leishmaniasis," Nagami wrote in her book *Bitten*, "but I knew that the American form, untreated, could eat up the middle of a person's face, starting with the nose. The Portugese in Brazil call the condition 'espundia,' or 'sponge.' That's what the person's face becomes—a ragged, porous hole, like a sea sponge."[8] Eliah did in fact have leishmaniasis, and after three weeks of medical treatment with lots of unpleasant side effects, he recovered.

Leishmaniasis is also a vector-borne protozoan disease that is transmitted through the bite of a small, mosquito-like fly called a sand fly. There are about twenty-one species of leishmania parasites that can cause disease in humans. It is most common in Africa, Asia, the Middle East, South America, and southern Europe. It is not normally seen in the United States. There are several forms of leishmaniasis, but the two most common are cutaneous leishmaniasis, which affects the skin, and visceral leishmaniasis, which invades internal organs such as the liver, spleen, and bone marrow.

People with cutaneous leishmaniasis, like Alfred Eliah, get skin sores that may show up weeks or months after the bite of an infected sand fly. The sores usually show up near the bite but may appear anywhere on the body. The sores may start out as bumps on the skin, but they can grow larger and become open and crusty. They can be very disfiguring, especially if they appear on the face. They can also appear in the mouth, nose, or throat. Treatment depends on the species of leishmania involved, the drugs that are available, and the severity of the sores. A drug called Pentostam is the most common medication. Smaller skin sores may not be treated at all, but healing without treatment can take years and leave scars.

People with visceral leishmaniasis may have symptoms such as fever, night sweats, abdominal pain, weight loss, blood abnormalities, and enlargement of the spleen or liver. It also damages the immune system by destroying white blood cells, which are necessary for fighting infections, so people with this form are much more susceptible to other infections such as pneumonia. Treatment most often includes an antibiotic called amphotericin, which is given directly into the bloodstream. If it is not available, an older drug called antimony may be used. Untreated visceral leishmaniasis is almost always fatal because of the damage it causes to the blood and the organs.

Toxoplasmosis

Toxoplasmosis is caused by a sporozoan parasite called *Toxoplasma gondii*. It is an extremely common infection among humans, currently affecting an estimated 60 million people in the United States alone. In some parts of the world, as much as 95 percent of the population may be infected. It is a major cause of death from food-borne illness in the United States.

Toxoplasmosis is most often spread in one of three ways—through contaminated food (especially raw or undercooked meat and raw goat's milk), from a mother to her unborn baby, and from cleaning or handling litter boxes or outside soil that has been contaminated with cat feces. Cats are the primary host for the Toxoplasma parasite. Cats pick up the parasite from eating infected birds or rodents. The parasite in cyst form is shed by the thousands or even millions in the cat's feces for up to three weeks after infection. People who handle litter boxes or

People who handle litter boxes or soil contaminated with cat feces and do not wash their hands afterward run the risk of getting a toxoplasmosis infection, which causes cysts in the mouth.

Toxoplasmosis and Schizophrenia

Schizophrenia is a very serious form of mental illness that causes a person to lose the ability to distinguish what is real from what is not. People with schizophrenia may have confused thinking and be unable to relate to other people and their surroundings in a normal way. They may speak in garbled sentences that make no sense. They may have hallucinations that cause them to see and hear things that are not real. They may have delusions that cause them to believe things that cannot possibly be true. Medications and psychological therapy can help control the symptoms of schizophrenia, but in more serious cases, if the individuals become dangerous to themselves or others, they may need to live in a psychiatric institution.

There are many theories about what causes schizophrenia. Some have to do with a person's genetics, such as having other family members with the disorder. Others focus on environmental factors, such as substance abuse or early emotional trauma. Another possible factor may be infection in the uterus before birth, including infection with the *Toxoplasma gondii* parasite that causes toxoplasmosis.

In a 2014 study Gary Smith, a professor of population biology at the University of Pennsylvania School of Veterinary Medicine, suggests that a significant number of schizophrenia cases may be caused by *T. gondii*. Smith used a complex set of calculations to try to determine how many cases of schizophrenia would likely not have occurred if there were no toxoplasmosis infections. His calculations showed that if toxoplasmosis infections could be stopped, as many as 20 percent of all cases of schizophrenia could be prevented.

soil contaminated with cat feces and do not wash their hands afterward run the risk of getting the cysts in their mouth and becoming infected.

If the person has a healthy immune system, he or she may not have any symptoms of toxoplasmosis and can recover from the infection completely. Unlike other parasitic diseases, once a person has recovered from toxoplasmosis, he or she will have immunity to it and will not get it again. If there are symptoms, they usually start out like mild flu—muscle aches, fever, swollen lymph glands, and so forth. The symptoms subside after a few weeks, but if the immune system is weak for any reason, such as being on chemotherapy for cancer or having AIDS, the parasite may remain in the body in an inactive state. If the person experiences any health problems that challenge his or her immune system, the parasite can become reactivated and cause problems such as damage to the eye or brain.

The most important danger of toxoplasmosis is that to an unborn child if the mother becomes infected during or just before her pregnancy. Unborn babies and newborns do not have a fully developed immune system, so they are very susceptible to the parasite. An estimated four thousand babies are born each year in the United States with signs of toxoplasmosis. Pregnant women and newborns can be treated with medications, but the treatment will not get rid of the parasite completely in either group because of the smaller dosage given to them.

Toxoplasmosis can cause miscarriage, fetal death, or skull malformation before birth, and vision loss leading to blindness, seizures, or developmental delays after birth. One woman, named Cynthia, writes:

> My mother was infected with toxoplasmosis in [the] first part of pregnancy. My twin was blind and severely brain damaged. She died at 9 months. I am blind in the left eye and limited vision in my right eye. I had small seizures until adulthood and out grew them. The toxoplasmosis became active again at 15 years old. Medication was successful and I retained my same vision. Able to attend normal schools and lead a fairly normal life with challenges.[9]

As dangerous as toxoplasmosis is, there is another sporozoan parasite that has been a major worldwide killer, especially of children, for many hundreds of years. It has killed more people than plague and smallpox combined. It is the parasite of the genus *Plasmodium*—the organism that causes malaria.

CHAPTER THREE

Malaria

In May 2010 Kelly Granger had just completed her freshman year at Davidson College in North Carolina when she left home to spend six weeks in the West African country of Ghana. The trip was part of a college program designed to immerse students in the daily life and culture of the country.

A few days after she returned home, she started to feel tired. She had headaches and fevers. Two days after seeing her doctor, her temperature went way up, and she began having chills and hallucinations. Her parents took her to the hospital, where the nurses noticed that her skin had become yellowish in color, a condition called jaundice that usually means something is wrong with the liver. Blood tests showed that Granger's red blood cells (the cells that carry oxygen to all the other cells in the body) were dangerously low and that her blood held high numbers of a protozoan parasite called *Plasmodium falciparum*. Granger was diagnosed with malaria, and of the four species of *Plasmodium* that cause malaria, *P. falciparum* is the most dangerous. She was put into the intensive care unit for treatment, where, after a rocky few days during which she ran very high fevers and slipped in and out of consciousness, she finally recovered enough to go home.

What Is Malaria?

Malaria is a mosquito-borne tropical disease that affects people and some animals. It is caused by parasitic protozoans belonging to the genus *Plasmodium*. There are more than one hundred species of *Plasmodium*, but only four cause malaria in humans. A fifth species infects macaque monkeys in Southeast Asia. Very rarely, people who live in close proximity to macaques may pick up this strain if they are bitten by a mosquito that has bitten an infected macaque. *P. falciparum*, the species that caused Granger's illness, causes the most severe cases.

Malaria is spread to people through the bite of several species of mosquito belonging to the genus *Anopheles*. Only the female mosquito can spread malaria because only the females take blood meals in order to prepare for egg production. Although the anopheles mosquito can be found all over the world (including the United States; eight U.S. presidents suffered from

The Anopheles Mosquito

Of the more than thirty-five hundred species of mosquito in the world, only thirty to forty species are able to carry the malaria parasite and transmit it to people. All of them belong to the genus *Anopheles*. Anopheles mosquitoes are found everywhere in the world except Antarctica. They can be distinguished from other species of mosquito by the black-and-white blocks on their wings and by their unique resting position—unlike other mosquitoes, anopheles mosquitoes hold their abdomens almost straight up in the air, rather than parallel with the surface. Most species are active from sundown to sunup.

Like most insects, anopheles mosquitoes have four stages to their life cycle—egg, larva, pupa, and adult. The first three life stages are aquatic, which is why mosquito control depends so heavily on eliminating sources of water in which adult females can lay their eggs. Males live for about a week, but females can live for two to four weeks. Only the females bite, since blood meals are required for them to produce eggs. After two to three days of rest, the female lays her eggs and then seeks another blood meal.

There are several reasons why the anopheles mosquito is uniquely able to carry malaria to people. First, other mosquitoes malaria), malaria transmission is most common in warmer tropical and subtropical areas of the world, closer to the equator, because the *Plasmodium* organism requires very specific conditions of temperature and humidity in order to complete its life cycle. For example, in temperatures below 68°F (20°C), *P. falciparum* cannot complete the part of its life cycle that takes place in the mosquito. Even in countries in which malaria is endemic (always present year-round), it may not appear in some areas of the country, such as at high altitudes or in dry desert areas.

Malaria is one of the most important of all global health problems; according to the World Health Organization (WHO), about 300 million to 500 million people get malaria each year,

have an immune response that makes it impossible for the malaria parasite to invade its gut wall, but the anopheles species that carry malaria lack this characteristic. Second, females live long enough for the parasite to complete that part of its life cycle in the mosquito. A third reason is that the anopheles species seem to have a strong preference for humans as their source for blood. This is especially true for the two most common anopheles species in Africa.

Malaria is spread to people through the bite of several species of mosquito belonging to the genus *Anopheles.*

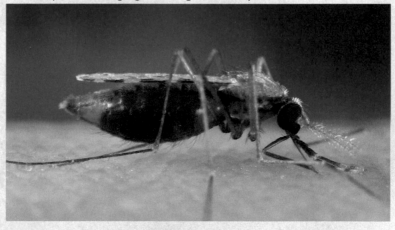

and between 1.7 and 2.5 million people die from it, including 3,000 African children under age five every day. In 2012 there were an estimated 207 million cases of malaria, with 627,000 deaths. In addition, approximately 10,000 to 30,000 travelers, like Granger, get malaria every year, and with increasing global travel, that number is rising. In addition, drug-resistant strains of *P. falciparum* have appeared, which makes treatment of the disease much more difficult.

An Ancient Disease

Malaria, or illnesses similar to it, has been known for more than four thousand years. The earliest writings about it come from a Chinese text called the Nei Ching Canon of Medicine, written about 2700 B.C. From ancient India comes the Susruta Samhita, a medical text dating from the sixth century B.C., which describes the symptoms and recognizes the role of insect bites in its transmission. Malaria was well known to the ancient Greeks; the renowned Greek physician-philosopher Hippocrates (c. 460 B.C.–c. 370 B.C.) wrote about its symptoms. The Greek conqueror Alexander the Great is thought to have died of malaria in 323 B.C. Ancient Roman writers believed the disease to be caused by foul air from swamps; the name *malaria* comes from the Italian words for "bad air."

Treatments for malaria have also been known for a very long time. In 340 B.C. a Chinese physician named Ko Hung wrote of the fever-reducing abilities of a plant called Qinghao. (In 1971 Chinese scientists isolated the active ingredient of Qinghao to create the antimalarial drug artemisinin.) When European missionaries arrived in the New World in the 1600s, they learned how the native peoples there used the bark of a tree, which the Europeans named *Chinchona*, to treat fevers. The highly effective antimalarial medicine quinine is still made from the bark of the *Chinchona* tree.

The ancient belief that malaria was caused by "bad air" remained until the late 1800s, when Louis Pasteur and Robert Koch were able to demonstrate that most infectious diseases are caused by specific microorganisms (the "germ theory" of disease). Once that discovery was made, new discoveries about malaria came rapidly. Early attempts to find a causative organism for malaria focused on looking at soil and water, but it was not found there. In 1880 French military physician Alphonse Laveran, who was stationed in Algeria, studied the blood of many of the French soldiers there who had contracted malaria. He eventually noticed and described small, dark bodies adhering to and destroying the red blood cells. He was convinced that these dark bodies were parasitic protozoans and that they were the cause of malaria. Where the parasites came from, however, and how they got into the blood, was still a mystery.

Two years earlier, in 1878, English physician Patrick Manson had demonstrated that the organism that causes the parasitic disease filariasis in people could be found in mosquitoes as well. "I shall not easily forget the first mosquito I dissected," he wrote. "I tore off its abdomen and succeeded in expressing the blood the stomach contained. Placing this under the microscope, I was gratified to find that, so far from killing the filaria, the digestive juices of the mosquito seemed to have stimulated it to fresh activity."[10] In 1897 another English physician, Ronald Ross, found malarial parasites in the gut of a mosquito that had fed on a person with malaria. He also discovered that the parasite spent a part of its life cycle there before traveling to the mosquito's salivary glands, where it could be transmitted to another person. The discoveries of Laveran, Manson, and Ross paved the way for the discovery of new ways to prevent and treat malaria.

The Life Cycle of the Malaria Parasite

During its somewhat complex life cycle, the malaria parasite infects two different hosts—female anopheles mosquitoes and humans. The parasite's life cycle begins when a female anopheles takes a blood meal from a person with malaria. When that happens, the mosquito picks up the parasites in the person's blood. At this early stage, the parasites are called gametocytes. This is a sexual stage; there are both male and

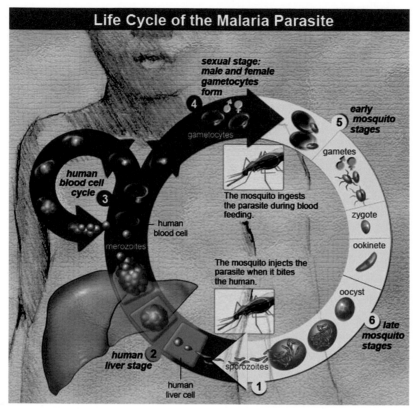

An Illustration of the life cycle of the malaria parasite. It first affects the liver and then attacks the red blood cells throughout the body.

female gametocytes. In the mosquito's gut, the gametocytes join together and form the next stage, called zygotes. The zygotes grow and invade the wall of the mosquito's gut. At this stage, they are called oocysts. The oocysts eventually rupture and release thousands of mature parasites called sporozoites. The sporozoites leave the mosquito's gut and travel to its salivary glands. When the mosquito bites another person, the sporozoites in the mosquito's saliva are injected into the person's bloodstream.

In the human the sporozoites travel through the blood and arrive, in just a few hours, at the liver (the liver stage). There they invade the liver cells, multiply rapidly, and eventually cause the liver cells to rupture, releasing the next stage, called merozoites. Each ruptured liver cell can release tens of thousands of merozoites. Some merozoites remain in the liver, where, if the disease is not treated, they can continue to multiply and cause flare-ups of symptoms for months or even years. Most of the merozoites, however, leave the liver and reenter the blood, where they invade the red blood cells (the blood stage). This is the stage in which the infected person begins to feel ill. In the red cells the merozoites multiply, eventually causing the red cells to rupture and release hundreds of new merozoites, which go on to invade and rupture more red cells. This cycle of multiplication, cell rupture, and reinfection of new red cells happens every one to three days, depending on the species of *Plasmodium* involved, and causes a sharp spike of fever every time. Some of the new merozoites enter the sexual stage and become male and female gametocytes. When the gametocytes are picked up by a feeding mosquito, the cycle begins again.

Symptoms of Malaria

Malaria causes illness by invading and destroying liver cells and red blood cells. Depending on the species of *Plasmodium* involved, symptoms usually begin from seven to thirty days after a bite from an infected mosquito. This incubation period may be longer in people who have had the disease before and recovered or in travelers who have received antimalarial drugs before traveling. *P. falciparum* has the shortest incubation period of the four disease-causing species. Early symptoms are the result of the body's immune response to the invading parasite and may include fever, chills, sweating, body aches, extreme fatigue, and headaches.

Symptoms of illness in the liver include abdominal pain, nausea and vomiting, liver enlargement, and jaundice. In the blood the widespread destruction of red blood cells causes a condition called anemia. Severe anemia can be life-threatening because there are not enough oxygen-carrying red cells to transport oxygen to the vital organs, especially the brain. In severe cases the lungs or kidneys may also be damaged by the parasite.

Malaria and Sickle-Cell Anemia

Sickle-cell anemia is an inherited disease in which an abnormal form of hemoglobin, the chemical that binds to oxygen in the red blood cells, is made. The abnormal hemoglobin can seriously damage the red cells, causing them to become rigid and sickle shaped instead of soft and rounded. A person must inherit a sickle-cell gene from both parents in order to have the disease. A person who inherits only one sickle-cell gene is said to have sickle-cell trait. A person with sickle-cell trait may have some sickling of the red cells, but his or her symptoms, if any, are much milder. Sickle-cell anemia is most common in people from tropical areas such as Africa, India, the Middle East, and Mediterranean or Caribbean areas.

In the 1940s British physician E.A. Beet noticed that African children with sickle-cell trait did not get malaria as often as children without the trait, nor did they suffer as much from the symptoms if they did get it. He discovered that their blood did not contain as many parasites as those without the trait. For reasons that are still not clear, *P. falciparum* does not survive as well in people with sickle-cell trait. It may be that sickle cells cannot carry enough oxygen for the parasites to survive, or it may be that because so many of the abnormal red cells are destroyed by the spleen there are not enough good red cells for the parasites to invade. Another possibility is that the sickle-cell trait changes the chemistry inside the cell in a way that is incompatible with the parasite.

Types of Malaria

WHO classifies malaria cases as either uncomplicated or severe. Uncomplicated malaria is characterized by malaria attacks— cycles of symptoms commonly called paroxysms. A typical paroxysm lasts about six to ten hours and consists of a period of feeling very cold with shivering, followed by a "hot" period of fever, headache, and vomiting, and then a period of sweating with a return to a normal temperature. Depending on the species of parasite involved, paroxysms may occur every two days, every three days, or in the case of *P. falciparum*, almost continuously.

Severe malaria is almost always caused by *P. falciparum*. In areas in which malaria is endemic, most victims of severe malaria are children who have never had the disease before and have no immunity. Most cases in other areas are seen in nonimmune travelers like Kelly Granger. Malaria is considered severe when other organs begin to fail or when anemia becomes so bad that the body cannot replace the lost red blood cells fast enough. Malaria is also considered severe if any one of a number of other symptoms listed by WHO appear. They include weakness so great that affected individuals cannot walk or feed themselves, convulsions, loss of consciousness, hypotension (very low blood pressure), blood in the urine or

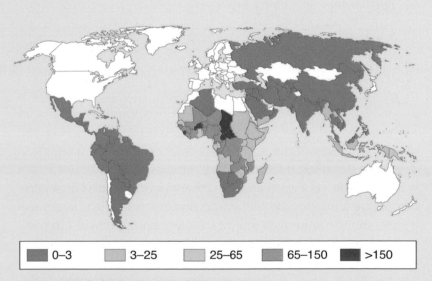

Malaria Death Rate per 100,000 Population

0–3   3–25   25–65   65–150   >150

Taken from: WHO World Malaria Report 2012. http://worldhealth.org.

stools, acidosis (high levels of acidity in the tissues), and fluid buildup in the lungs. Cerebral malaria is a very serious complication that occurs when damaged red cells cling to the sides of the blood vessels in the brain and block blood flow. A person with cerebral malaria may show abnormal behavior, loss of consciousness, multiple seizures, coma, and eventually death.

Ann Paisley Chandler, a Peace Corps volunteer working in West Africa, endured a bout of severe malaria despite having taken preventive drugs before her travels. She says:

> At the end of my tour . . . I became sick with malaria while traveling in Italy. My "flu-like" symptoms, not treated, led to anemia, disorientation, hypotension, toxic shock, hallucinations, double pneumonia, blood transfusions, 24-hour kidney dialysis, [being on a ventilator] due to acute respiratory distress syndrome, a feeding tube, coma, and all of my organs shutting down one by one. According to my Italian doctors, a 5–10% chance of survival.[11]

Chandler was very lucky to have survived her extreme case of malaria. A person who survives a case of malaria will have some immunity to future infections. If he or she gets it again, the symptoms are usually milder.

Diagnosis and Treatment of Malaria

Once symptoms begin, malaria progresses very rapidly. For this reason, and in order to prevent further spread of the disease, prompt diagnosis is extremely important. Diagnosis of malaria is based on the patient's travel history, symptoms shown, and blood tests that show anemia, lower-than-normal blood-clotting ability, and higher-than-normal amounts of bilirubin, a chemical that indicates liver and muscle cell damage. The definitive result is the presence of *Plasmodium* parasites in the blood. The higher the parasite load in the blood, the more severe the disease will be. A parasite load of just 5 percent is enough to kill about 20 percent of patients. Chandler's parasite load was 22 percent.

Treatment of malaria depends on the severity of the disease; the particular species of *Plasmodium* involved; other health is-

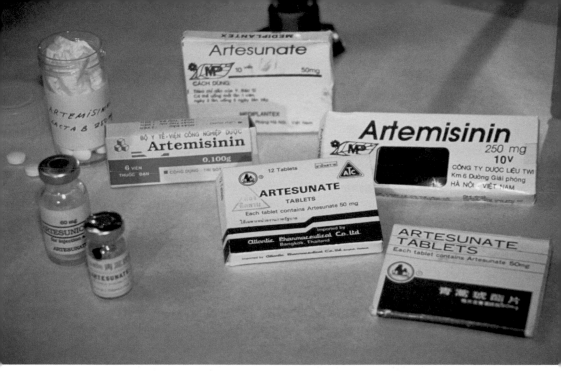

There are many antimalarial drugs on the market. They include quinine, chloroquine, primaquine, mefloquine, and artemisinin.

sues the patient may have, such as pregnancy, heart disease, or kidney disease; and the area of the world in which the disease was acquired. Admission into a hospital, if one is nearby, is essential. An intravenous (IV) line is started to keep the patient hydrated and to administer antimalarial drugs and antibiotics. Antimalarial drugs work by killing the parasite in all of its life stages. They include quinine, chloroquine, primaquine, mefloquine, and artemisinin. They can be given orally or through the IV, but the IV route is preferred if the patient cannot keep pills down or if the malaria is severe. The choice of which drug to use depends on the species involved and whether it is resistant, or immune, to any of the drugs.

Other kinds of measures may become necessary if the disease becomes severe and starts to affect other organ systems. Blood transfusions may be given to combat anemia. Dialysis may be necessary if the kidneys fail. A ventilator may be needed if the patient cannot breathe adequately on his or her own. Recovery from malaria can take weeks or months. Even after recovery is complete, any parasites remaining in the liver can cause flare-ups of symptoms for years afterward.

Preventing Malaria

Prevention of malaria centers on preventive medications, eliminating mosquitoes, and preventing mosquito bites. The drugs used to treat malaria also help prevent the spread of the disease to others. They can also be given to people who plan to travel to malaria-endemic areas. Although these drugs do not guarantee that a person will not get malaria, they can help minimize the parasite load and reduce the severity of the symptoms if a person does become infected.

Reducing the numbers of mosquitoes can be done in several ways. One way is to eliminate standing water in which mosquito larvae develop. Another way, used in some countries, is to coat interior walls with insecticides such as dichlorodiphenyltrichloroethane (DDT). An infected mosquito that lands on a treated wall to digest its blood meal will pick up the insecticide and die before it can bite someone else.

Preventing mosquito bites is commonly done by using insect repellents such as DEET on the skin and clothing, and by wearing long pants and long sleeves to reduce the amount of exposed skin for mosquitoes to bite. Another highly effective way is to use insecticide-treated mosquito nets in endemic areas. Mosquitoes tend to be most active at night, and using bed nets to cover and surround beds from sundown to sunup has been shown to prevent bites by as much as 70 percent compared to no net.

Malaria in the United States

Until the early 1950s malaria occurred naturally in the United States, especially in the southern states, where the climate is warm and well suited for mosquitoes. In 1942 the Office of Malaria Control in War Areas was established in Atlanta, Georgia, to try to limit the impact of malaria on southern military training bases. After World War II the office became the Centers for Disease Control and Prevention, and efforts were begun to eradicate, or eliminate, malaria from the United States altogether. Strategies included the use of the insecticide DDT in rural areas, including on the inside walls of homes, and drainage of swamps and other areas of standing water in which mosquito larvae

Preventing mosquito bites can be done by using insect repellants such as DEET or other products on the skin and clothing and by wearing long pants and long sleeves to reduce the amount of exposed skin for mosquitoes to bite.

grow. These efforts were very successful, and in 1949 malaria was eliminated as a national health concern. By 1952 the CDC was no longer involved with malaria in the United States.

Today, according to the CDC, an average of about fifteen hundred cases of malaria are reported in the United States each year. Almost all of these are brought in by travelers, mostly from tropical areas of Africa in which malaria is endemic. In 2011 there was a spike in malaria cases; 1,925 cases were reported that year, the highest in forty years. The most likely reason for the spike included travelers not taking antimalarial drugs before travel and military personnel bringing it back from endemic areas.

Malaria and the Panama Canal

Within fifty years of the discovery of the New World, European powers recognized the advantage of having a way for ships to get from the Atlantic Ocean to the Pacific Ocean without having to sail all the way around South America. Ideas for a canal across the Central American country of Panama were proposed, but the technology to build such a canal was not available until the late 1800s. Having successfully completed the Suez Canal in Egypt in 1869, the French were the first to make such an attempt. Construction began in 1881, but several major problems—including mountainous terrain, floods, mudslides, and illness from malaria and yellow fever—put a stop to the project in 1889. By then more than twenty-two thousand workers had died of disease.

In 1902 the canal project was taken over by the United States, and in 1904 the Panama Canal Zone was signed over to the U.S. government and became a U.S. territory. By this time the connection between malaria and mosquitoes had been discovered, and disease control became a high priority. Sanitation commissions headed by chief medical officer William Gorgas were created to oversee disease control. Hospitals and quarantine facilities were built, and screens were put on the workers' living quarters. Gorgas's "mosquito brigades" managed mosquito elimination efforts such as draining swamps, oiling the surface of ponds and lakes, killing mosquito larvae, and fumigating to kill adult mosquitoes. These efforts were hugely successful; no deaths from yellow fever occurred in the Canal Zone after November 1906, and by 1910 the death rate from malaria had dropped to less than 1 percent. Today the Panama Canal area is still free of malaria and yellow fever.

William C. Gorgas supervises swamp removal at the Panama Canal. He eradicated the malaria-bearing mosquitoes in Panama.

Three species of the anopheles mosquito live in the United States, and there have been occasional cases in which a person in the United States has contracted malaria from being bitten by a mosquito that has bitten an infected traveler. Between 1957 and 2011, sixty-three outbreaks of malaria occurred in the United States this way. An average of four people in the United States die from *P. falciparum* malaria each year.

There are several other ways that malaria can be transmitted in the United States. "Airport malaria" is transmitted by mosquitoes from endemic countries that manage to get on an airplane and travel to other countries, where they can infect people. Although uncommon (two cases were reported in 2011), it is possible for a pregnant woman with malaria to transmit the disease to her unborn baby during pregnancy or delivery. Another uncommon method of transmission is through blood transfusions. According to the CDC, between 1963 and 2011 there were ninety-seven cases of malaria transmitted in this way. There is no screening test for malaria in donated blood, so donors must answer detailed questions about their travel history before being accepted for donation.

CHAPTER FOUR

Helminths

In 2008 a fifty-year-old British man of Chinese descent began experiencing an unusual set of worrisome symptoms, including headaches, seizures, memory problems, and unusual smells. After four years and many tests, the cause of the symptoms was still a mystery. Eventually, he was diagnosed with a brain tumor. During a biopsy of the tumor, performed in 2012, a small piece of tissue was removed. After examination in a lab, the tissue was found to be not a tumor at all, but rather a piece of a parasitic worm, or helminth, which had been living inside the man's brain for four years. During that time, the worm had traveled about 2 inches (5 cm) through the man's brain, causing the unusual collection of symptoms. The species of worm was identified as one that is fairly common in Far Eastern countries such as China, Japan, Korea, and Thailand. The man most likely picked up the parasite during one of his many trips to China. The worm was removed and the man recovered.

What Are Parasitic Helminths?

Parasitic helminths are worms that can infect humans, other animals, and even some plants. In people and animals, helminths most commonly live inside the intestinal tract of the host animal, although some helminths infect other organs as well. The helminth that infected the man from England and settled in his brain was a tapeworm, one of the three main groups of helminths. Helminths are are quite diverse, encompassing thousands of different species ranging in size from tiny filarial worms to tapeworms that can reach several yards in length. Almost all vertebrate animals, including people, serve as hosts to helminths at some time in their lives.

Helminths are far more complex organisms than protozoans. They are multicellular and have several body parts. They are bilaterally symmetrical, which means they look the same on the right and left sides of their bodies (like people). They are invertebrates, which means they have no backbone, and they have no skeleton. Some have inner body cavities for digestion, and some do not. They have no true respiratory or circulatory systems, but they do have well-developed reproductive systems.

The Helminth Life Cycle and Transmission

Most helminths pass through three stages during their life cycle—egg, larva, and adult. Eggs are produced by an adult female. One helminth can produce thousands of eggs every day. Once released from the adult worm's body, the eggs are

Helminths are a very diverse group of parasitic worms, comprising thousands of different species ranging in size from tiny filarial worms to tapeworms that can reach several yards in length. An adult male and female parasitic worm of the genus Schistosoma are shown here.

expelled into the environment through the host animal's intestinal tract in its feces. (One exception to this cycle are the filarial worms, which are transmitted to people by mosquitoes and do not live out in the environment.) When conditions of temperature and moisture are right, the eggs hatch into the larval stage. Sometimes the eggs hatch while still inside the host and are expelled as larvae.

Most helminths do not spend their entire life cycle in the human body. During its larval stages, the parasite may remain in the environment, or it may develop inside the body of another

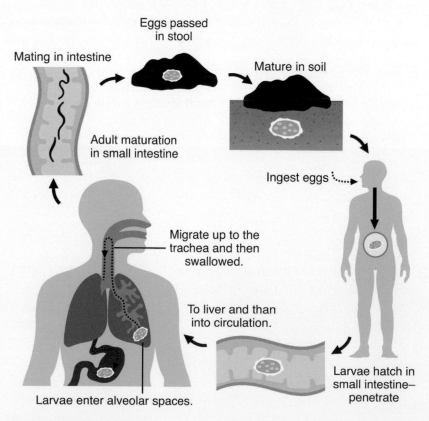

Helminth Life Cycle

Eggs passed in stool

Mating in intestine

Mature in soil

Adult maturation in small intestine

Ingest eggs

Migrate up to the trachea and then swallowed.

To liver and than into circulation.

Larvae enter alveolar spaces.

Larvae hatch in small intestine— penetrate

Taken from: Centers for Disease Control

animal before infecting a human. The host in which the mature adult parasite lives, mates, and produces eggs is called the definitive, or primary, host. Humans are the definitive host for many helminths. Other animals that may serve as hosts during the larval stages are called intermediate, or secondary, hosts.

A helminth can be transferred to a new host in several ways, depending on the species. The simplest is the fecal-oral route, in which the eggs or larvae are expelled in the feces of one host, then get picked up by another by eating unwashed or undercooked food or by drinking contaminated water. In the transdermal route, larvae in the soil penetrate the skin of the host and migrate through its body until they reach the intestinal tract. Some helminth larvae are transmitted by insect vectors through the bite of an infected mosquito or fly. People can also pick up helminth infections by eating other animals that are infected, such as snails, beef, or pork.

Helminths are generally classified according to their body shape, which may be round or flat in shape. Round-bodied worms are called nematodes (from the Greek *nemato*, which means "thread"). Flat-bodied worms are called platyhelminths (*platy* means "flat"). The flatworms are further divided into two groups—cestodes, or tapeworms; and trematodes, or flukes.

Nematodes (Roundworms)

Nematodes, or roundworms, are the single most abundant animal on the earth. Approximately 80 percent of all animals on the planet are nematodes. Approximately twenty thousand species of nematode have been identified, but nematode experts believe there are thousands more yet to be identified. About sixty species are parasitic to humans.

Nematodes have long, thin, bodies with a tubular internal digestive cavity that runs the length of the body. A mouth opening at the front end lets them take in food, and an opening at the back lets them expel waste products and, in females, eggs. The internal cavity is filled with fluid and helps support and provide some rigidity to their soft bodies.

Adult nematodes are either male or female. After mating, the female produces eggs, which are passed out of the female's

Helminthic Therapy and the Immune System

The human immune system is responsible for recognizing, attacking, and destroying harmful foreign substances such as bacteria, viruses, and parasites and is triggered when these threats, called antigens, get into the body. The immune system has evolved over many thousands of years to be most effective when it is regularly exposed to harmful antigens from an early age. If it is not exposed regularly, it can malfunction, become overactive, and begin to attack the body's own tissues instead. The illness that results is called an autoimmune disease.

There are about seventy-five different autoimmune diseases, including asthma, bowel diseases such as Crohn's disease, rheumatoid arthritis, eczema, celiac disease and other food allergies, and multiple sclerosis. Over the past hundred years, autoimmune diseases have become much more common in modern, industrialized areas of the world. This may be at least partly due to greatly reduced exposure to biological antigens because of improved sanitation, hygiene, and antibiotic use. Helminths have been an important part of the evolution of the human immune system. Their natural presence in the body over tens of thousands of years helped establish a balance in the internal human environment. In areas of the world where helminth infections are still common, autoimmune diseases are not common.

Helminthic therapy is an alternative way of treating autoimmune diseases that involves deliberately infecting a person with helminth eggs or cysts in order to stimulate the immune system in a normal way and get it to stop attacking normal tissues. The most common helminths used are pig whipworms, human whipworms, hookworms, and rat tapeworms. Helminthic therapy is experimental and has not yet been fully approved for use in any country. However, research in several countries, including the United States, has shown promising results, especially with the use of hookworm.

body and into the host's intestinal tract. From there, the eggs are passed out into the environment. The larvae of the nematode develop inside the eggs until the temperature and moisture are right for hatching. After hatching, the larvae feed on bacteria in the environment and grow until they become mature enough to infect a new host, either an animal or a person. During the final phase of growth inside its host, a nematode becomes either male or female. Mating occurs, eggs are produced, and the cycle begins again.

Cestodes (Tapeworms)

Cestodes, or tapeworms, look very different from nematodes. Tapeworms have long, flat bodies that are divided into segments called proglottids. They can grow to be extremely long; some tapeworms have been measured at almost 60 feet (18m) long! Tapeworms have an organ at their head end called a scolex. The scolex contains special structures that help tapeworms attach to the inside of their host's intestine. Once they are attached, they live on the digested food particles that pass by them. They do not have an inner digestive cavity at all but take in nutrients by absorbing them through the outer layer of their bodies, called the tegument. Carbon dioxide and other waste products of metabolism diffuse out of their bodies the same way. Tapeworms do not have any kind of circulatory, respiratory, or nervous system.

Behind the scolex is a neck area where new proglottids are formed. As each new proglottid is formed, the older ones are moved back, and eventually a long chain of segments is created. Larger tapeworms may have several thousand segments!

Unlike nematodes, cestodes are not separated into male and female. Instead, each mature proglottid contains both male and female reproductive organs and can produce both eggs and sperm. Sperm cells produced in one proglottid can fertilize eggs produced in the proglottids of the same worm or of other worms. A single proglottid can produce tens of thousands of eggs. The eggs leave the host's body when older proglottids near the end of the worm break off the chain, break open, and

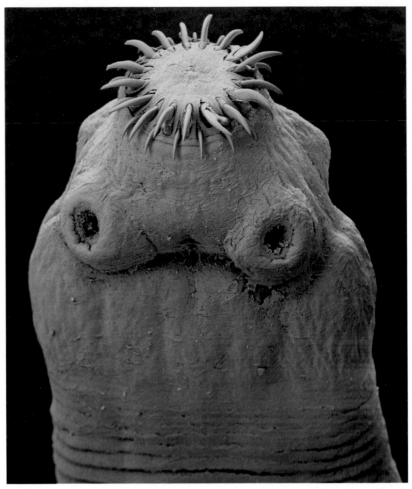

A tapeworm has an organ at its head end called a scolex that allows the tapeworm to attach to the inside wall of its host's intestine.

release the eggs, which are passed out through the host's feces into the soil or water.

When cestode eggs are consumed by an intermediate host such as a cow or a pig, they hatch into the larval stage. After a period of growth, the larvae burrow into the animal's muscle and form a rigid protective cyst around their body. If a human eats the meat of an infected animal, the larvae become active and attach themselves to the human's intestine, where they live and grow into mature adults.

Trematodes (Flukes)

Trematodes are commonly called flukes. They have small, flat, leaf-shaped bodies with suckers at their front end and on their belly to help them attach and hang on to their host's intestine or other organs. They range in size from less than 0.125 inches (3mm) to about 3.5 inches (9cm).They have a pouch-like gut but no true body cavity. Flukes are classified by what part of the body they infect. There are blood flukes, liver flukes, lung flukes, and intestinal flukes.

Trematodes complete their life cycles in two different hosts, an intermediate host (almost always freshwater snails) and a definitive host, either humans or other vertebrate animals such as pigs, cows, rats, dogs, monkeys, and others. Like tapeworms, most adult flukes are hermaphroditic, which means each fluke has the reproductive organs of both sexes. (Schistosomes are the exception—they have separate male and female sexes.) The mature fluke produces eggs that, like other helminths, are

Trematodes have small, flat, leaf-shaped bodies with suckers at their front end and on their bellies to help them attach and hang on to their host's internal organ.

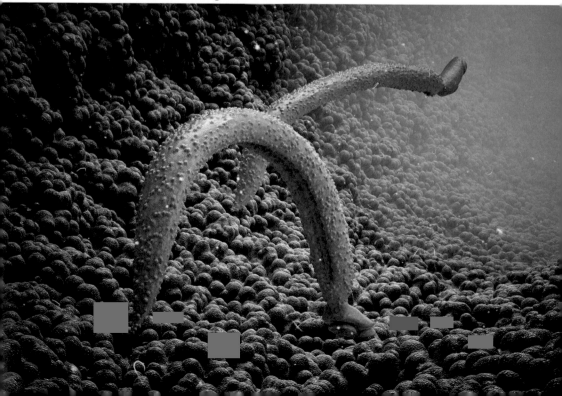

expelled from the definitive host's body into the environment. Eggs that get into water hatch into tiny larvae. In the water the larvae find a snail of the right species for that particular kind of fluke. They penetrate the snail's body and live on the snail's body tissues. As they grow inside the snail, they develop a tail that allows them to swim. The larvae then leave the snail and return to the water. If a human enters the water, fluke larvae can penetrate the person's skin and travel through the blood-stream to the lungs, liver, or intestine, where they live as adults and start the life cycle again. They can also get into a human if an infected snail is eaten.

Helminth Infections

Helminth infections are among the most common infections in the world. Like most parasitic diseases, they are most commonly seen in tropical areas of Africa, Asia, and South America, where the climate is warm and humid, and in poorer, more remote areas where sanitation, food preparation, and personal hygiene practices are inadequate. They may also be seen during the warmer months in areas that are farther from the equator and have cooler climates, including Europe and the United States.

Unlike protozoans, which develop very quickly inside the host, helminths develop rather slowly, and they may live for years inside their host. For these reasons, symptoms tend to show up gradually and can last for a long time. Many helminth infections may not show any symptoms at all. Others, however, can cause serious or life-threatening illness. Because their eggs and larvae are passed out of the host, the number of worms inside a host at any given time and the severity of the disease they cause depend largely on how many eggs or larvae a host picks up. The symptoms a person has depend on the particular worm involved, the part of the body affected, and how long the person has been infected.

Diagnosis of a helminth infection is made on the basis of the symptoms the patient is having and through microscopic examination of the blood and/or stool for the presence of para-sites or their eggs. The size, shape, and structure of helminth eggs varies according to the particular worm involved. For example, some helminth eggs are operculated (o-PER-cue-lated), which means they have a sort of "cap" at one end that opens when the egg hatches. Some helminth eggs are oval, others

How Do They Live So Long?

Parasitic flatworms such as tapeworms and flukes are known for their ability to live for decades inside their human hosts. Scientists at the University of Illinois, led by biologist Phillip Newmark, believe they have discovered one secret to flatworms' long lives—stem cells.

Stem cells are immature, nonspecialized cells that have the potential to become any kind of specialized cell. Stem cells are found in all multicellular animals, including people. In a developing embryo, stem cells can develop into any kind of organ or tissue cell. In adult organisms, stem cells repair and replace old or damaged cells.

Scientists already knew that stem cells called neoblasts exist in planarians, which are nonparasitic flatworms. These neoblasts can become any kind of cell that the planarian needs and can even be used to regenerate body parts that have been cut off. Newmark and his team wondered whether parasitic flatworms also had neoblasts that could repair their tissues and help them live for so long. For their study they used schistosomes, the blood fluke that causes schistosomiasis. Using a special technique for tagging dividing cells, they found groups of dividing cells in the worm's body that were not already part of any of the worm's organs. They injected the tagged cells into mice infected with schistosomes and found that the cells ended up in the intestine and muscle tissue of the schistosomes in the mice. This told them that the tagged neoblasts had in fact become specialized schistosome cells.

Scientists studying stem cells in parasitic flatworms believe that this research may lead to new ways to treat flatworm infections by destroying their stem cells and shortening their life spans in people.

are shaped like lightbulbs, and others are barrel shaped. Some have thick, dark shells, and some have thinner, clear shells. All these characteristics help doctors identify the parasite if no adult worms are seen in the sample.

Ascariasis

"One day not very long ago," writes Albert Marrin in his book about parasites called *Little Monsters*,

> a researcher sat at her desk at the United States National Parasite Collection in Beltsville, Maryland. She had just returned from Egypt and was eager to study the specimens she had collected there. As she leaned over to look into her microscope, she felt an odd tickling sensation. Moments later, a nine-inch worm slid out of her nose. . . . Most likely, it was the giant roundworm, *Ascaris lumbricoides*. Yet she was lucky, since this species gets to be 13 inches long, and she had just one. Some people have hundreds of these worms wending their way through their bodies.[12]

Ascariasis (as-car-EYE-asis), caused by the ascarid worm, is the most common helminth infection in the world. It is estimated that more than 1 billion people have ascariasis, most of them children in sub-Saharan Africa, Asia, and Latin America. Like most helminth diseases, infection occurs by eating food or drink contaminated with ascarid eggs. Ascarid eggs can remain alive in the soil for several years.

The ascarid worm is the largest nematode that infects humans; the females of one ascarid species can grow up to 16 inches (41cm) in length. Males are slightly smaller. A female ascarid worm can produce more than two hundred thousand microscopic eggs each day. Once ingested, ascarid eggs hatch in the intestines. The tiny larvae burrow through the wall of the intestine and migrate through the blood to the lungs. Eventually, they get into the trachea, or windpipe, where they are coughed up and swallowed. The larvae then pass through the stomach again and settle in the intestine, where they become adult worms.

Ascarid infections often show few or no symptoms. Mild abdominal pain with or without diarrhea is the most common symptom. As the larvae penetrate the gut wall and migrate through the body, they can cause breathing problems and inflammation of the abdominal cavity or the lungs. The adult worms living in the intestines can cause malnutrition by stealing nutrients from food eaten by the host. If the infection is very heavy, it can cause growth retardation in children, blocked intestines, and damage to the liver, pancreas, or spleen. Left untreated, heavy ascarid infections can be fatal.

Hookworm

Hookworm is another very common nematode infection, affecting up to one-fifth of the world's population. The hookworm gets its name from the hook-like bend at its head end. Hookworms are much smaller than ascarids, growing to only about 0.5 inches (1.3cm) long. Hookworms have well-developed mouths with cutting plates or "teeth" that allow them to fasten themselves to the intestinal wall of their host.

Hookworms attach themselves to the inner lining of the intestines.

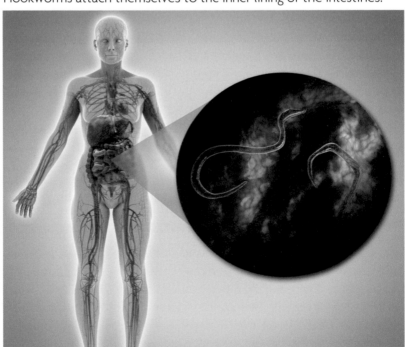

Like with ascarids, hookworm disease is a soil-transmitted disease. It is common in tropical and subtropical areas and is usually spread through direct contact with soil that has been contaminated with infected feces. After the eggs are deposited into the soil, they hatch into larvae. After about ten days, the larvae become infective. If a person walks barefoot in contaminated soil, hookworm larvae can burrow through the skin on the feet or legs. When the larvae arrive at a small blood vessel, they migrate through the bloodstream and travel up to the lungs, through the airways, and into the back of the throat. When the infected person coughs, the larvae are swallowed and travel into the small intestine, where they attach themselves to the intestinal wall. There they mature into adult worms and feed on the blood of their host.

Symptoms of hookworm infection are usually mild but can become severe if the person becomes heavily infected. One of the earliest signs is intense itching with a rash, called "ground itch," at the site of skin penetration. Once the larvae get into the lungs, they can cause a cough that may or may not include coughing up blood. In the intestine they usually do not cause symptoms, although some people may have diarrhea, abdominal pain, or nausea. Because hookworms feed on the host's blood, over time they can cause anemia (loss of red blood cells), which can be especially dangerous for children, pregnant women, and people with illnesses.

Lymphatic Filariasis

Lymphatic filariasis (fil-ar-EYE-asis) is an infection caused by a small, slender nematode belonging to a group of nematodes called filarial worms. The disease affects more than 120 million people in tropical areas of sub-Saharan Africa, Asia, and parts of South America. It does not exist in the United States. Lymphatic filariasis is different from most other nematode infections in that it is not spread through contaminated soil, but by mosquito bites. Several species of mosquito serve as intermediate hosts for the parasite, including the anopheles mosquito that carries malaria.

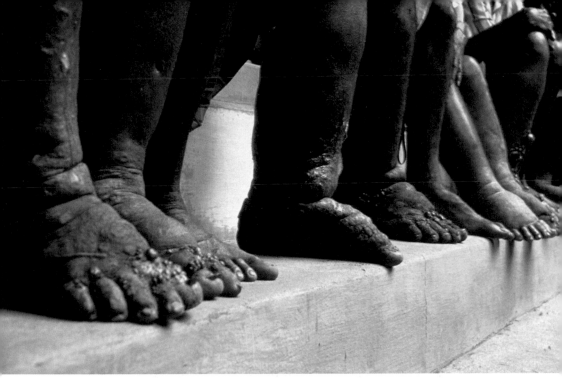

People with swollen legs due to severe lymphatic filariasis, commonly known as elephantiasis.

Humans are the definitive host for the parasite. After mating, the adult female worm produces millions of microscopic larvae called microfilariae. When a mosquito bites an infected person, the microfilariae enter the mosquito's body and spend part of their lives developing there. When the same mosquito bites another person, the microfilariae migrate into the person's lymphatic system, where they mature into adult worms.

Many people with lymphatic filariasis do not show symptoms and may not even know they are infected. When symptoms occur, they are caused by the damage the worm does to the lymphatic system. The lymphatic system is part of the circulatory system. It consists of a network of organs, tissues, and vessels that carry a clear liquid called lymph. The lymphatic system has several important functions, including carrying excess fluid out of the body's tissues and carrying white blood cells to the sites of infections. When the lymphatic system is unable to remove excess fluid in the body's tissues, a condition called lymphedema results. Lymphedema causes severe swelling, most often in the legs, but it can also affect the arms, breasts, or genitalia, especially the scrotum in men.

People with lymphatic filariasis may also get other infections more easily, especially skin infections. Over time, these skin infections can cause the skin to become thickened and tough. The combination of thickened skin and extreme lymphedema is commonly called elephantiasis because its appearance resembles the legs of an elephant. Elephantiasis is very disfiguring and disabling, and it can prevent people from being able to work or care for their families. Many are shunned by their communities because of their appearance. Unfortunately, medications for treating filariasis cannot reverse elephantiasis because the damage to the lymphatic system has already been done.

Tapeworm Infections

Humans are the definitive host for tapeworms. Six species of tapeworm are known to infect people, but the most common ones are the pork tapeworm and the beef tapeworm. Infection occurs when a person eats undercooked meat from an infected intermediate host, such as a cow or a pig. The tapeworm larvae live inside the animal's muscle inside a protective cyst. When the larval cysts get into a human's intestine, they open up. The larvae leave the cyst and attach to the inside of the human's intestine, where they grow into adults and begin to reproduce. Pork tapeworm eggs can also be transmitted by eating food that has been prepared by an infected person who has not washed his or her hands.

Beef tapeworms rarely kill people, but because they rob the host of so many nutrients, the infected person may lose weight and become weak, and may also experience abdominal pain, nausea, and diarrhea. These symptoms are usually mild, and a person may have the infection for his or her entire life and never know it. If the tapeworms grow very large, however, they can block the intestine. They may also block ducts, or tubes, that lead from the gall bladder or pancreas and carry digestive fluids into the intestine. Surgery may be necessary to treat this problem.

An infection with the pork tapeworm can be much more dangerous. Pork tapeworm larvae are able to migrate out of the intestine and into organs such as the lungs, brain, liver, or even eyes. If that happens, the larvae form cysts in the organ. This is called cysticercosis (sis-ti-ser-KO-sis). Over time the cysts may grow large enough to interfere with the function of the organ or with its blood supply. The cysts may also rupture, which releases more larvae that can move to other organs and form more cysts. When this happens in the brain, it is especially dangerous. The person may experience headaches, dizziness, vision problems, seizures, dementia, inflammation of the brain (encephalitis), or fluid collection in the brain (hydrocephalus). This kind of tapeworm infection is the most common cause of seizures in children living in underdeveloped countries.

Fortunately, treatment of most tapeworm infections is relatively easy. The medications used are not absorbed by the intestine, so they are very effective at killing the adult tapeworms. When the killed tapeworm is passed from the body, it is important to make sure the head and scolex are out, because if they are not, the worm can regrow itself. Cysticercosis is more difficult to treat. In addition to medications, surgery or even an organ transplant may be necessary, depending on the organ involved.

Schistosomiasis

Schistosomiasis (shis-to-som-EYE-asis), also called bilharzia (bil-ARE-zee-a), is caused by a blood fluke called a schistosome. It is estimated that more than 200 million people are currently infected with this parasite worldwide, and that more than two hundred thousand people die each year in Africa alone from complications of schistosomiasis. Like most helminth infections, it is most common in poor, underdeveloped areas of Asia, Africa, and South America. Women and children who work or play in infected water are especially at risk for infection. There are two major types of the disease—urogenital, which affects the bladder, kidneys, and reproductive organs; and intestinal, which affects the bowel and liver.

After leaving the body of their intermediate host, the freshwater snail, schistosome larvae get into the human body by penetrating the skin of the legs or feet. Once inside the human host, they get into the bloodstream, where they live and mature into adult flukes. The adult female produces eggs that travel through the blood to the intestines or bladder. Some of the eggs are passed out of the body in the urine or stool. Others remain the body and become embedded in the bladder or intestine. In rare cases they can also get into the brain or spinal cord.

Mobile Phone Microscopy

Today's mobile phone technology can let the user do almost anything. An online article published March 11, 2013, in the *American Journal of Tropical Medicine and Hygiene* describes a way for scientists and doctors in remote areas to diagnose helminth infections using their mobile phone as a microscope.

During a trial of an antihelmintic drug in Tanzania, researchers used double-sided tape to attach a tiny, spherical lens over the camera lens in a mobile phone. They held the phone very close to microscope slides containing thin smears from stool samples. They also looked at the samples using a regular microscope. Overall, the phone microscope was not quite as accurate as the regular microscope at detecting the presence of helminth eggs or at demonstrating what species of eggs they were. It was most accurate (81 percent accuracy) at detecting ascarid eggs. It did not do as well for detecting hookworm, and it also gave some false positive results (detecting eggs where there were none).

The researchers understand that mobile phone microscopy is not yet nearly accurate enough for regular use in the field. However, mobile phones are portable, easy to use, inexpensive,

The symptoms of schistosomiasis appear a few days after infection and at first are caused by the body's immune response to the presence of the eggs, rather than by the flukes themselves. Early signs may include a rash or itch, fever, or muscle aches. Children who get multiple infections may suffer from slow growth, learning problems, malnutrition, and anemia. Over many years schistosomiasis can cause inflammation and damage to the bladder, kidneys, intestine, or liver. Chronic symptoms include abdominal pain, liver enlargement, diarrhea, or blood in the urine or stool. It can also increase the

and can be found almost everywhere. So researchers feel certain that, with improved technology, mobile phone microscopy will become a valuable tool for use in the future.

A smart phone equipped with an acrylic lens shows an enlarged image of a fly's leg.

risk of bladder cancer. Infection in the brain can cause seizures or paralysis.

Treatment and Prevention of Helminth Infections

Treatment for helminth infections most often involves medications. The medication chosen depends on the species of helminth that is diagnosed. The first line of medication treatments are antihelmintic drugs. They are designed specifically to rid the body of worms. Some of them kill the worm right away. Others paralyze or stun the worm, which eventually leads to its death. The most common antihelmintics are albendazole and mebendazole. They are especially effective for nematode infections such as hookworm. Antihelmintics can also be taken before traveling to underdeveloped areas as a preventive measure.

Other drugs used for helminth infections include antibiotics and steroids. Antibiotics such as tetracycline and doxycycline are often used for filarial worm infections because they kill bacteria that live symbiotically inside the worm and seem to have a role in the worm's reproduction. Some people may experience an extreme immune response to the worm infection or to the dead worms after treatment. Symptoms of an overly strong immune response include high fever, severe muscle pain, tissue swelling, and shock; these can be worse than the worm infection itself. Steroids may be used to control such symptoms.

The best ways to prevent helminth infections all involve minimizing the chances of helminth eggs or larvae getting into the body. The single most important method of prevention is thorough hand washing with clean, hot water and soap before eating, after taking care of a sick person, after using the bathroom, and after handling animals or soil. Food precautions include washing raw fruits and vegetables thoroughly with clean water, thoroughly cooking meats and seafood, avoiding unpasteurized dairy products and juices, and eating food prepared by others only if it has been prepared properly. Drinking water is safest if it is commercially bottled or thoroughly boiled before using it in food preparation. Wearing shoes at all times helps prevent infection from hookworms and flukes that can penetrate the skin. Insect repellent and mosquito nets are helpful for minimizing insect bites that transmit filarial parasites.

Another important focus for preventing soil-transmitted helminth infections involves providing effective sanitation methods. For example, in many poor, remote areas of the world, people may have no bathrooms or toilets and are forced to use roadside ditches or even open fields for this purpose. Sanitation measures such as functioning latrines could help prevent this kind of soil and water pollution. A 2012 Swiss study found that people who had access to latrines and used them were about 50 percent less likely to get a helminth infection than those who did not have access to them. "Cure alone is almost useless in stamping out hookworm disease," say the authors of the study, "because the patient can go out and immediately pick up more hookworms. The cure should be accompanied by a sanitation campaign for the prevention of soil pollution."[13]

CHAPTER FIVE

Ectoparasites

Protozoan and helminth parasites are endoparasites, which means they live inside their host's body. Ectoparasites are parasites that live on the outside (*ecto* means "outside") of their host's body, generally on or in the skin of the host. Almost all vertebrate animals (mammals, birds, fish, amphibians, reptiles) are affected by ectoparasites of one kind or another at some point in their life. Most ectoparasites are arthropods, either insects or arachnids. The most common human ectoparasites are fleas, ticks, mites, some flies, and lice.

Parasitic Arthropods

Most parasitic relationships involve arthropods in some way, either as parasites themselves, hosts for other parasites, or vectors for a protozoan or helminth parasite. Some species, such as fleas and ticks, are hematophagous, which means they feed on the blood of their host. Others, such as botfly larvae, are histophagous, which means they bite or burrow into the skin and feed on tissue cells.

Arthropod parasites have separate male and female sexes. After mating, the female produces eggs, which hatch into larvae. Some species, such as botflies, are parasitic in the larval stage, but others are not. As the larvae grow, they go through a process called metamorphosis, during which their bodies change from the larval stage into the adult stage. Some species go through complete metamorphosis, in which the larva encases itself in a hard shell called a pupa. When it emerges from the pupa as an adult, it looks completely different from the larva. A familiar example of complete metamorphosis is seen in flies and butterflies as they transform from maggots or caterpillars into winged adults. Other species go through incomplete metamorphosis. They do not form a pupa but hatch from the egg looking like a small version of the adult, called a nymph. As it grows into an adult, the nymph molts, or sheds its exoskeleton, several times.

Parasitic arthropods are generally transmitted from host to host in one of two ways—direct transmission or host-seeking transmission. In direct transmission the larvae, nymphs, or adults of fleas, mites, and lice jump or climb directly from one host animal to another, or their eggs or pupae may be picked up from close contact between hosts or by people sharing clothing or bedding. Winged parasitic insects such as flies actively seek hosts either to feed on them or deposit eggs so that their larvae can feed on the host. Ticks also seek out hosts by climbing onto plants and waiting for a host to pass by.

Botfly larvae (shown) go through a process called metamorphosis, during which their bodies change from the larval stage into the pupal stage.

Fleas

Fleas are wingless insects with hind legs that are especially adapted for jumping from host to host or from the ground to a host. Fleas can jump as much as one hundred times their body length. Fleas are not parasitic in their larval stage, but as adults they feed on the host's blood. Some flea species spend only a short time on their host and drop off after they are full. Others spend their entire adult lives on their host. Most species of fleas do not cause disease themselves but serve as vectors for other disease-causing organisms such as cat scratch disease and typhus. One of the most famous flea-borne diseases is bubonic plague, a deadly bacterial disease carried by a particular species of flea that parasitizes rodents and humans and has caused untold millions of deaths throughout human history.

It is possible for people to get tapeworm infection from fleas. One species of tapeworm uses fleas as an intermediate host. Flea larvae on the ground pick up tapeworm eggs that have been shed in the feces of a dog or cat. The eggs hatch into larvae inside the flea and live there as the flea becomes an adult. If the flea is accidentally ingested by a person—which is more likely in an infant or young child who spends a lot of time on the ground—the tapeworm larvae can get into the person's intestine.

Tungiasis (tun-GUY-asis) is a disease caused by a species of parasitic flea called the chigoe flea, also called sand fleas or jiggers (not to be confused with chiggers, which are mites). These fleas are found in Central and South America, Africa, and India. At only 0.04 inches (1mm) in size, they are the smallest of the fleas. Adult fleas live in dirt or sand. After mating, the female chigoe flea burrows headfirst into the skin of its host, a human or other mammal, usually on the toes, feet, or lower legs. It then feeds on the tiny blood vessels in the lower layers of the skin. Over the next two weeks, as its eggs develop, its body swells to about the size of a pea. This creates a bump or nodule in the skin, with a tiny hole in the top through which the chigoe breathes. After two weeks the flea releases forty to fifty eggs through the opening in the skin. The eggs fall to the ground and hatch after three or four days.

Tungiasis causes extreme itching and pain in the affected areas. Damaged areas of the skin can become ulcerated and infected with other diseases such as tetanus and gangrene. Treatment for tungiasis may include removing the flea with forceps, killing the flea by "freezing" the nodule with liquid nitrogen, antiparasitic medicines, antibiotics, or surgery to remove dead tissue.

Parasitic Flies

In the summer of 2014, biologist and entomologist (insect scientist) Piotr Naskrecki traveled to Belize in Central America to photograph the plants and animals there. The area was thick with mosquitoes, but he did not let that stop him from journeying into the jungle to take his pictures. "When I returned home," he writes, "I noticed that some of my mosquito bites were not really healing. I also noticed that something was living in them. I had the human botfly."[14]

Flies are not truly parasitic to humans as adults, although several species of flies bite humans and feed on human blood, such as mosquitoes, horseflies, deerflies, and sand flies. Some adult flies can transmit other parasitic diseases to people, such as malaria, elephantiasis, and African sleeping sickness. Botflies and screwworm flies are two species of flies that are actually parasitic to humans in their larval stage. Infestation with fly larvae is called myiasis.

Human botflies are found in southern Mexico and Central and South America. They are large, hairy flies and look somewhat like bumblebees. They are colorful, with bright blue abdomens and large, bright red eyes. The female botfly prefers to lay her eggs on the bodies of mosquitoes or other flies and use those insects as an intermediate host to carry the eggs to a mammalian host such as a person. After hatching, the tiny botfly maggots drop off the insect when it lands on a person.

Once on the host, the maggots burrow under the skin, causing painful, pus-filled blisters called warbles. Botfly maggots have many backward-facing spines on their bodies that help them stay in the skin. During this time they feed on the

Using the "Birds and the Bees" to Fight Flies

Screwworm flies are no longer a problem in North America, largely because of a technique that uses the fly's own biology as a control method. The technique is called sterile male release, or sterile insect technique. Using this technique, male flies that have been sterilized with gamma radiation are released into the environment in such large numbers that fertile male flies cannot compete with them for females. After mating with sterile males, the female lays infertile eggs that cannot hatch into maggots.

Sterile male release was pioneered in the 1950s by American entomologists Raymond Bushland and Edward Knipling. In 1954 it was used to eradicate screwworms from the island of Curaçao, just north of Venezuela. In 1959 about two billion sterilized male flies were released in parts of Florida over eighteen months. The program was so effective at eliminating the flies from Florida that similar programs were done in several southwestern states and along the U.S. border with Mexico. By 1966 there were virtually no screwworm flies left in the United States. In 1972 sterile male release was used in Mexico, and by 1991 screwworms had been eradicated from that country as well. The technique is currently being used in Central American countries and has eliminated screwworm flies from all but three countries there.

Screwworm flies were the first pest to be controlled using sterile male release. This technique is also proving to be successful for controlling other kinds of insects such as several species of fruit flies and the African tsetse fly, which spreads the parasitic disease African sleeping sickness.

skin and grow to be 0.5 to 1 inch (1cm to 2cm) long. After four to eight weeks of growth, they emerge from the skin, drop to the ground, and form a pupa. A week later they emerge as adult flies.

Treatment for botfly infection may include suffocating the maggots with petroleum jelly or wax and removing them with tweezers, removing them surgically, or using antiparasitic medication to kill them. Maggots have also been removed by using a snake venom extractor to suck them out. Antibiotics are given to prevent infection in the wound. Naskrecki removed one of his three botfly larvae with a venom extractor but decided, out of curiosity, to allow the two remaining ones to live in his skin so he could observe them as they matured. After nearly ten weeks, the larvae emerged from his skin. He put them in a container of soil and observed them as they pupated and finally emerged as adult flies. He even made a video of the entire process, which is available on line. (Warning— high gross-out factor!)

Screwworm flies are found in Central and South America. After mating, the female screwworm fly lays approximately four hundred eggs on the skin of a warm-blooded host, usually on an open wound or other break in the skin such as a tick bite. A common site is the unhealed navel of a newborn. The eggs hatch within hours of being laid, and the larvae begin feeding

The female screwworm fly lays approximately four hundred eggs on the skin of a warm-blooded host, usually on an open wound or other break in the skin, such as a tick bite.

immediately, using hook-like mouthparts to tear the tissue. If they are disturbed, the larvae just burrow deeper into healthier tissue, including muscle, and feed on that as well. As the wound created by feeding larvae grows larger, other females may come along and lay their eggs there, too. The wound may become infected, which attracts other species of flies whose larvae feed on dead tissue. After several days of feeding, the larvae drop to the ground to pupate. After about a week, the adult flies emerge from the pupa. Treatment for screwworm infestation is similar to that for botfly, with removal of the maggot and antibiotics to prevent wound infection.

Lice

Lice are wingless insects that spend their entire lives on their hosts, and they are parasitic at all stages of their life. Lice have no eyes and cannot jump, but they do have claws on their legs designed for clinging. They are small, from 0.05 to 0.125 inches (1 to 3mm). Each day, the female louse lays three to four eggs, which are called nits, on the skin and hair of the host and cements them there, using a kind of "glue" that comes from her reproductive organs. After the eggs hatch into nymphs, they cling to the hair or skin as they grow and molt on their way to adulthood.

Some lice feed by chewing or biting the skin. Others are sucking lice and feed on blood. Infestation by blood-sucking lice is called pediculosis. The lice that infect people are blood-sucking lice and bite four or five times every day to feed. Three kinds of sucking lice are parasitic to humans, depending on the part of the body on which they live. Body lice live anywhere on the body and prefer to lay their eggs in clothing. Head lice live in the hair on the head, and pubic lice, or crabs, live in the hair of the pubic area.

Lice are spread directly from person to person through close body contact or by sharing personal items such as clothing and hats, beds, or hairbrushes and combs. They are more common among those who live in unsanitary living conditions but will infest anyone, given the opportunity. Head lice in particular

The female head louse lays three to four eggs each day, which are called nits, on the skin and hair of the host and cements them there with a glue-like secretion.

can become a problem in schools, spreading quickly from child to child. Girls are infested more often than boys, possibly because they are more likely to share clothing and hairbrushes.

Symptoms of lice infestation include intense itching of the infected area, rash, and allergic reactions to the bites. Persistent scratching can cause tears and sores in the skin, which can become infected. Head lice and pubic lice do not transmit other diseases and are considered more of a hygienic nuisance than an actual health hazard. The body louse, however, can spread the bacterial diseases typhus, trench fever, and relapsing fever.

These three diseases can cause high fevers with delirium, headaches, muscle pain, rashes, falling blood pressure, nausea, and
vomiting.

Lotions that kill adult lice and their nits are used to treat
pediculosis. Special fine-toothed combs can be used to remove
nits and dead lice from the hair. Shaving the head will get rid
of nits and adults, but it is a drastic measure and not really
necessary. Clothing, bedding, and personal items should be
thoroughly cleaned to get rid of eggs. Extensive housecleaning
is not usually necessary because lice cannot live more than a
day without feeding.

Ticks

When Albert Marrin was a boy, he lived in New York City in a
crowded apartment building. Fortunately for Marrin, there was
a park within walking distance that had a large wooded area
where he and his friends would play a game they called "Jungle."
It was there that he had his first experience with a parasite:

A tick attached to the hair follicles of its host.

Once, as I got ready for bed after a long day of Jungle, I noticed several tiny brownish things clinging to my legs. They had hard shells, and felt like seeds. Yet, when I tried to brush them off, they did not budge. Instead, they seemed to tighten their grip with sharp tongs. It hurt. 'Ticks,' said the emergency room doctor at the local hospital. 'Your boy has ticks,' he told my father.[15]

Ticks are tiny eight-legged arachnids that live on the blood of birds and mammals. There are almost nine hundred species of tick. They can be found in many parts of the world but prefer warmer, more humid climates in order to reproduce. There are two main groups of ticks—hard ticks, with a rigid exoskeleton, and soft ticks, which have a more leathery exoskeleton. Hard ticks are more commonly found on people than soft ticks. They have a hard outer shield called a scutum, which is what makes these ticks so difficult to crush. They also have a feeding apparatus called a hypostome, which has barbed "teeth" on it and which they use to attach themselves firmly onto the skin of their host.

The life cycle of the tick can last a year. Females lay several thousand eggs on the ground. When the larvae (which have only six legs) hatch, they feed on small mammals and birds. After feeding, they drop off and molt into nymphs. As the nymphs grow into adults, they feed on larger animals such as people.

Ticks cannot jump or fly, so they must seek out hosts. Using their back legs, they cling to a leaf or blade of grass and wait for an animal or person to pass by. This is called questing. They can sense the presence of a possible host animal by detecting their breath, body heat, odor, or movement. When a person or animal walks by, ticks climb or drop onto it and begin to seek skin to which they can attach themselves. They use their mouthparts to cut a tiny hole in the skin. They insert the hypostome and begin feeding on the host's blood. As they feed, their body becomes engorged with blood. When they are full, they drop off the host onto the ground.

Tick bites themselves are usually harmless. Some people may have an allergic reaction to the tick saliva and experience pain, swelling, a rash or blister, or in rare cases, difficulty breathing. The real danger of tick bites is that they can spread other serious disease-causing pathogens, including bacteria, viruses, or other parasites, to people. One tick can carry more than one pathogen at a time, and tick eggs can become infected with pathogens before they are even laid. Tick-borne illnesses are the most common vector-borne illnesses in the United States. More than a dozen tick-borne illnesses have been identified. With about twenty thousand to thirty thousand cases reported each year since 2002, the most common by far is Lyme disease.

Lyme Disease

A Minnesota woman tells about her experience with Lyme disease:

> I've got a place in the north woods of Wisconsin—a cabin that I go to every weekend, if possible—and I think that's probably where I got the tick bite. One day in my adventures up there I just started feeling really bad. Really sleepy—I didn't quite feel right. . . . It got so bad that I finally went to the doctor. I had a heck of a fever—103.2, if I remember correctly! And during my visit they determined I did indeed have Lyme disease.[16]

Lyme disease is a bacterial infection spread to people by the deer tick, one of the smallest species of ticks and most common in northeastern and north-central states. Symptoms begin within seven to ten days of the bite, with an expanding red rash around the bite. As the rash expands, the central part of it clears up, leaving a ring-shaped rash. Other symptoms include fever, headache, muscle and joint pain, and swelling of the lymph nodes in the groin or neck. Early symptoms usually go away without treatment in about three weeks, but they can come back.

Lyme disease is dangerous because, later in the course of the disease, it can affect the nervous system, with symptoms such as meningitis (an inflammation of the membrane covering of the brain and spinal cord), nerve inflammation, weakness, or loss of reflexes lasting as long as ten years. It can also damage the heart and cause inflammation of the heart muscle or

Tick-Borne Viruses

Most tick-borne illnesses are caused by various species of bacteria and can be treated with antibiotics. In June 2014 a farmer from Bourbon County, Kansas, named John Seested began to feel ill, with symptoms typical of a tick-borne illness—high fever, severe headache, loss of appetite, muscle aches, nausea, and fatigue. When his symptoms got worse, he was taken to the hospital, where he tested negative for all the usual tick-borne diseases. None of the standard antibiotic treatments for tick-borne illnesses worked, and after ten days he died from multiple organ failure. Six months later, researchers from the University of Kansas and the CDC determined that the illness had actually been caused by a virus, which is why the standard antibiotic therapies did not work. The virus was identified as being genetically similar to one that is seen in African and Asian countries but had never been seen in the Western Hemisphere before. The disease was named Bourbon virus, after the name of the county where the patient lived.

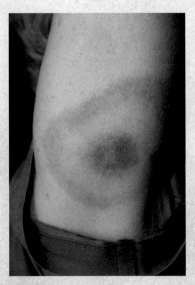

Bourbon virus is similar to another uncommon tick-borne virus named heartland virus, which first appeared in 2009 and which so far has sickened ten people in Missouri, Oklahoma, and Tennessee, two of whom died from the disease. Currently, there is no specific treatment or cure for these viruses.

The bull's eye rash is a common symptom of tick-borne Lyme disease.

rhythm abnormalities. Some people develop a form of arthritis that comes and goes and can last as long as several years. Early Lyme disease can be treated with antibiotics, but long-term symptoms do not often respond to treatment.

Other Tick-Borne Diseases

Other tick-borne illnesses not as common as Lyme disease include babesiosis (ba-beez-ee-OH-sis) and tularemia (too-la-REEM-ia). Babesiosis is also spread by deer ticks and can be transmitted together with Lyme disease in one tick bite. It is caused by a parasitic protozoan that invades the red cells, and its symptoms are similar to malaria. Like Lyme disease, it is most common in the Northeast and Midwest. Symptoms are usually mild and include fatigue, loss of appetite, fever, muscle aches, and sweats. Many people have no symptoms at all. The danger of babesiosis is that it weakens the immune system. If a person who already has a weak immune system due to age or other illnesses also gets Lyme disease, it can cause severe, long-term illness, with kidney failure, anemia from loss of red blood cells, and dangerously low blood pressure. People with mild symptoms usually do not require treatment. If symptoms are severe, it can be treated with malaria drugs such as quinine, along with antibiotics.

Tularemia is also called rabbit fever. Most cases occur in the southern Midwest. There are two forms of the disease. The milder form begins with a sore at the site of the bite, fever, and swollen lymph nodes. These symptoms may go away on their own, or they may progress to a more severe form of the disease, with high fever, chills, severe headache, abdominal pain, and profound fatigue. Tularemia is also treated with antibiotics.

Tick-borne illnesses can cause serious problems, with long-term symptoms and disability. Because their symptoms resemble influenza and other common illnesses, an accurate diagnosis can be missed and treatment delayed. The best way to avoid getting a tick-borne disease is to use insect repellent on the skin and clothing and to wear long pants and long

How to Remove a Tick

It is important to remove ticks from the skin as soon as they are discovered. If the tick has attached itself to the skin, it can be difficult to get it out, but according to the CDC, a simple pair of fine-tipped tweezers is effective for removing ticks, if it is done correctly.

First, use the tweezers to grasp the tick as close to the skin as possible. Then, using steady, even pressure, gradually pull the tick upward until it lets go. Do not twist it or try to jerk it out; this may cause the body to separate from the mouthparts, leaving them in the skin.

If this happens, try to remove the mouthparts with the tweezers. If this is not possible, leave them alone and keep the area clean. Eventually, they will fall out on their own. After removing the tick, clean the bite area and the hands with rubbing alcohol, an iodine scrub, or soap and hot water. Dispose of the tick by putting it in alcohol or a sealed bag or container, wrapping it in tape, or flushing it down the toilet. Never crush a tick with the fingers, because there may be pathogens in the tick's body that can be spread if the tick is crushed.

Do not try to make the tick drop off by "suffocating" it with nail polish or petroleum jelly, and do not try to kill it with a hot match. Folk remedies such as these are not reliable, can be dangerous, and can take too long to work when the goal is to get the tick off as soon as possible. If symptoms of a tick-borne illness appear after a bite, see a doctor and be sure to mention the bite.

sleeves when outdoors, especially in the warmer months. Clothing should be washed in hot water and dried in a drier. A hot shower helps remove ticks that have not attached themselves to the skin yet. The skin should be closely examined, especially around the feet, ankles, legs, and head, and any ticks removed immediately.

Mites

Mites are near-microscopic arachnids. Like ticks, their eggs hatch into six-legged larvae that molt into eight-legged nymphs. There are more than thirty thousand species of mites. Most are nonparasitic or are parasitic to birds, fish, reptiles, other mammals, and amphibians. They will, however, parasitize people if their preferred host is not available. Two kinds of mites are especially annoying to people—chiggers and scabies.

Chiggers are actually the larval form of a family of mites called Trombiculidae. Chiggers are almost microscopic in size.

Chiggers attach themselves to a young girl's feet. Chiggers are not transferred from person to person, and contrary to popular belief, they do not burrow under the skin.

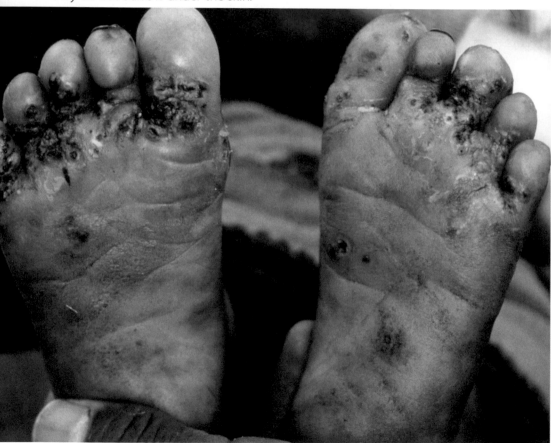

They are red and have six legs like other arachnid larvae. They need a moist environment in which to live, so they are most often found close to the ground on plants or in the grass. Chiggers get onto people when people walk through the woods or sit in the grass. The chiggers then move over the skin looking for a good place to bite. They prefer to settle wherever the skin is the thinnest and where they are least likely to be disturbed, such as the armpits, groin, navel, or behind the knees. They also tend to settle and bite around areas of tighter-fitting clothing, such as under socks or the waistbands and leg openings of underwear, because this stops them from moving any farther on the skin. Chiggers are not transferred from person to person, and contrary to popular belief, they do not burrow under the skin. Rather, they insert their mouthparts into the skin and inject a chemical that breaks down the skin tissue. In this way they create a tiny tube-like structure called a stylostome and feed on the destroyed skin cells. If they are not disturbed, they may stay there for several days. The stylostome is what causes the intense itching and red, raised bumps of chigger bites. Treatment is aimed at relieving the itching and inflammation. Calamine lotion or anti-itch steroid creams can be used, or oral medications such Benadryl may be used.

Scabies is a skin disease caused by a mite called the itch mite or scab mite. Itch mites are different from chiggers in several ways. First, itch mites are transmitted from person to person by direct skin contact, especially by hugging or through sexual contact, so scabies can be a very contagious disease. Second, they spend their entire life cycle on their host, not just their larval stage. Third, female itch mites do burrow into the skin after mating, using their mouthparts and special cutters on their front legs. As she moves through the skin, she creates a tunnel and lays eggs in it, two or three each day. After hatching, the larvae come out of the skin and settle around hair follicles, where they feed and molt until they become adults.

The presence of the burrowing mites creates an intensely itchy rash made up of red bumps and blisters. The presence of the eggs can cause a severe allergic reaction, which makes the itching even worse. The itching of scabies tends to start out mild, but over a few weeks it becomes much worse, especially at night, and does not stop. Because itch mites remain in the skin, treatment is designed to kill the mites as well as relieve the itching. Prescription lotions and anti-itch medications are used. Clothing and bed linens must be washed, and people who have had close physical contact with infected persons should be treated as well.

CHAPTER SIX

Parasitic Diseases Today and in the Future

"**N**owhere is it more true," wrote nineteenth-century German zoologist Rudolf Leuckart, "that 'prevention is better than cure,' than in the case of parasitic diseases."[17] Throughout human history, parasitic diseases of all kinds have caused untold suffering, countless deaths, and enormous social and economic damage in all areas of the world. Today parasites and the illnesses they cause continue to impact humanity in these ways. However, because these diseases are largely illnesses of the poorest and most remote areas of the world, there has traditionally been little attention paid to them by developed countries—those that have the greatest financial and technological ability to help fight them. For this reason, several of the most common parasitic diseases are considered "neglected" diseases by WHO.

Neglected Tropical Diseases

WHO has identified a group of eighteen diseases that are called neglected tropical diseases. Of the eighteen NTDs, eleven of them are caused by protozoan or helminth parasites, and of these eleven, six are transmitted to people by arthropod ectoparasites such as flies or mosquitoes. One, scabies, was just added to the list in June 2014. These diseases are considered neglected because, although they continue to cause tremendous suffering in the poorest parts of the world, they receive relatively little international attention or financial support for research, control, and treatment. According to Carlos M. Morel of WHO, "It has been estimated that less than 10% of global spending on health research is devoted to diseases or conditions that account for 90% of the global disease burden."[18] Much more financial support has been dedicated to diseases that are known to kill more people and are more in the public awareness, such as tuberculosis, HIV/AIDS, and malaria. Most NTDs already have established control measures and effective treatments, such as water-treatment and sanitation measures, insect control, and medications (many of which are donated free by pharmaceutical companies), but these measures are often not available in poorer areas where they are most needed.

According to the CDC in Atlanta, Georgia, NTDs kill approximately 534,000 people each year. They are endemic, or always present, in 149 countries, most of which are in Africa, Asia, and Latin America. In the countries in which NTDs are the most prevalent, they cause high rates of school absenteeism, lost worker productivity and wages, and a tremendous financial burden on governments. Some of them, such as lymphatic filariasis, cause disfigurement that can cause affected people to be socially isolated and unemployable. The CDC explains:

> Affecting the world's poorest people, NTDs impair physical and cognitive development, contribute to mother and child illness and death, make it difficult to farm or earn a living, and limit productivity in the workplace. As a result, NTDs trap the poor in a cycle of poverty and disease. More than 1 billion people—one-sixth of the world's population—suffer from one or more Neglected Tropical Diseases.[19]

Despite these obstacles, research continues in many parts of the world in order to learn more about the diseases themselves and the most effective ways to prevent, control, and treat them. Organizations such as WHO and the CDC are very active in the fight against NTDs. For example, WHO has established a coordinated database for storing information and data about NTDs from many sources so that countries can make better decisions about what kinds of programs to establish and how best to spend their limited health-care resources. "This integrated database will enable us to manage large amounts of data and greatly improve the management of information transmitted

Lymphatic filariasis, often called elephantiasis, infects the lymphatic system and causes great swelling, such as of this woman's leg.

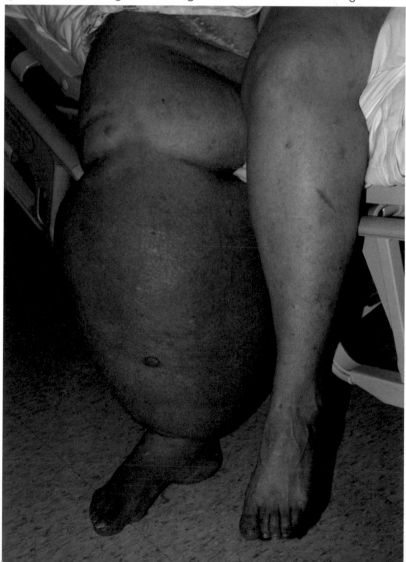

from sub-national levels to national levels," says physician Pamela Sabina Mbabazi. "It will also assist in strengthening our ability to store and share data."[20]

WHO and the CDC, along with other health organizations and drug companies, have also established global programs directed toward controlling and eliminating specific NTDs, including parasitic diseases such as lymphatic filariasis (elephantiasis), river blindness, schistosomiasis, and soil-transmitted helminth infections. These programs have been

Closing in on Victory— Eradicating Guinea Worm

In 1980 the deadly disease smallpox was declared officially eradicated, or eliminated, from the world. Now another disease is close to becoming the second human disease to be eradicated. Guinea worm disease is a waterborne parasitic helminth disease that occurs in Africa and once occurred in Asia. It is on WHO's list of NTDs.

Once ingested, guinea worm larvae grow in the body for about a year, after which time pregnant adult females emerge from the body through painful blisters, most often on the legs or feet. At 2 to 3 feet (61 to 91cm) in length, it can take several weeks for the worm to get all the way out, and it is very difficult to walk or work during that time because of the pain. If the person tries to ease the pain by putting the affected part in water, the adult female senses the temperature difference and releases thousands of new larvae into the water. The blisters can easily get infected with bacteria, which can make the person very ill.

In 1986 the Carter Center, established by former U.S. president Jimmy Carter, took on the task of eliminating guinea worm. Efforts were directed toward educating people about the disease and how it is contracted and providing water filters for filtering the highly successful for several diseases. For example, river blindness has been eliminated in ten West African countries and in eleven of thirteen areas in Latin America in which it was endemic. Since 2007 lymphatic filariasis has been eliminated from China and Korea, and its transmission has been interrupted in several Caribbean countries. It is estimated that approximately 6.6 million newborns worldwide are now protected from getting this debilitating and disfiguring disease.

parasites out of drinking and cooking water. Since the effort began, guinea worm cases have dropped from about 3.5 million in twenty countries in 1986 to only 148 total cases in 30 villages in South Sudan, Mali, Chad, and Ethiopia. There are so few cases now that all those who have it have been identified and are being treated so that it cannot spread any further, and it is expected that guinea worm will be declared eradicated in a few years. The success with guinea worm shows what can be achieved through dedicated education and prevention.

In July 2004 Carter Center volunteers assemble medical kits to be shipped to Africa, where the guinea worm has been nearly eradicated.

Neglected Parasitic Infections in the United States

Parasitic diseases are most commonly thought of as diseases that affect poor countries in other parts of the world. However, parasites are a major problem in the United States as well. Neglected parasitic infections are a group of five parasitic diseases that have been identified by the CDC as priorities for public health intervention in the United States, based on the number of people infected, the severity of the illness they cause, and the availability of effective prevention and treatment methods. They include Chagas' disease, cysticercosis (caused by the larval form of the pork tapeworm), toxocariasis (a disease caused by the larvae of a roundworm that infects dogs and cats), toxoplasmosis, and trichomoniasis. They are considered neglected because relatively little attention has been devoted to them even though they affect millions of people in the United States. More than 60 million people are thought to be currently infected with toxoplasmosis alone.

Efforts to control these infections exist both in the United States and other countries. For example, programs to control toxoplasmosis infection, which can have devastating consequences for newborn babies, include screening pregnant women for infection and preventing infection through education for women. Toxocariasis can damage the liver or lungs and can cause blindness, especially in children, but little research has been done on this disease. The CDC is working to increase knowledge about this disease so it can be better controlled. The occurrence of Chagas' disease, which has traditionally been seen mostly in Mexico and Central and South America, has been rising in the United States. Efforts to control this potentially deadly disease include collecting data about who gets Chagas' disease and where it is occurring, screening blood donors and pregnant women for the parasite, improving diagnosis, and educating the public about Chagas' disease and the insects that transmit it.

Controlling Malaria

Of all the parasitic diseases caused by protozoans, malaria is by far the deadliest. Malaria was essentially eliminated from the United States in 1951, but it continues to exact a huge toll in terms of illness, death, and financial burden in many parts of the world. According to the CDC, "Malaria caused an estimated 207 million cases and 627,000 deaths in 2012, mostly young children in sub-Saharan Africa. It contributes to poverty; in Africa alone, costs of illness, treatment, and premature death from malaria are at least $12 billion per year."[21] Costs of preventing and treating malaria take up about 40 percent of health spending in African countries where it is most common. For families, it takes up about 30 percent of household income in terms of treatment and lost wages from the illness or death of wage earners.

In Africa, where malaria has its biggest impact, the disease has been difficult to control. High numbers of anopheles mosquitoes in Africa carry the deadly *P. falciparum* species of the parasite. The climate there is ideal for both of these organisms. Many of the poorer countries in sub-Saharan Africa do not have good infrastructure, such as roads and bridges, to bring supplies and medicine to outlying population areas. In addition, these poorer countries often cannot afford the costs involved with malaria control.

The ultimate goal of malaria control is to eliminate the disease altogether in endemic areas and eventually to eradicate it, or eliminate it, worldwide. The shorter-term goal of malaria control in most countries is to reduce as much as possible the number of deaths caused by the disease, especially among children. These goals are considered possible because of increased international attention and commitment on the part of national governments and health agencies since about 2000. These efforts have focused primarily on several specific areas: case management, which means diagnosing and treating as many cases as possible, distributing mosquito nets that have been treated with insecticides, preventing malaria in infants and pregnant women, and insect control and elimination.

Diagnosis and treatment can be difficult in endemic areas because malaria symptoms can be similar to other diseases, and many countries lack the sophisticated equipment needed to make an accurate diagnosis. In addition, health-care workers are often undertrained and overworked, and there are not

Drug Resistant Malaria

One of the most pressing problems in the fight against malaria is the appearance of strains of the malaria parasite that have developed resistance, or immunity, to standard antimalarial drugs. Three of the five known species of *Plasmodium* are known to have this resistance, including *P. falciparum*, the most dangerous of the five. Resistance to the drugs means that the parasite is not completely removed from the patient's blood after treatment, so it can easily flare up again.

Organisms such as bacteria and viruses are able to modify their own genetics, after repeated exposure to the drugs used to treat them, in ways that make them resistant to the drugs. A well-known example is methicillin-resistant *Staphylococcus aureus*, or MRSA, which was traditionally treated with the antibiotic methicillin but has become resistant to it. Viruses are especially good at changing their own genes, which is why there are so many different strains of influenza virus and why the annual influenza vaccine is different every year. Drug-resistant malaria first showed up in the late 1950s and has now developed resistance to almost all of the currently available malaria drugs, including artemisinin, the most effective of all antimalarials.

In 2001 WHO developed a plan for addressing this problem through increasing efforts to contain the spread of resistant strains of malaria, expanding measures already in place to control malaria, and stepping up research into new antimalarial drugs. One promising new drug is simply called SJ733. This molecule actually triggers the body's immune system to destroy infected red blood cells, disrupting the parasite's developmental cycle while leaving healthy cells alone. By targeting infected cells rather than the parasite itself, the problem of drug resistance is avoided. It also works very quickly; in mice one dose was enough to make the parasite undetectable in the blood after only forty-eight hours.

enough of them to handle the caseload. Since 2000 more rapid diagnostic test kits and modern microscopes have been made available, along with more trained personnel, making diagnosis and treatment easier and more effective.

Pregnant women who have had malaria and are somewhat immune to future infection may lose some of that immunity during pregnancy, which makes them more susceptible to infection than other immune adults. Malaria can cause anemia in the mother and premature delivery, low birth weight, and death of the baby. Pregnant women and young children (most of whom have never had malaria and have no immunity) are provided with insecticide-treated mosquito nets (ITNs) and treated with medications to avoid anemia and prevent infection.

ITNs have been shown to be highly effective at preventing malaria cases. The nets not only provide a barrier for people, especially at night when mosquitoes are most active, they also kill insects that land on them and keep them out of homes. If even half the people in a community use ITNs, the whole community can be better protected because the population of insects is decreased. Several companies have developed ITNs that can last for up to three years before the insecticide wears off, even with regular washing. Between 2008 and 2010 almost 300 million nets were distributed to people in sub-Saharan Africa.

Reducing the numbers of anopheles mosquitoes is a crucial part of controlling malaria. One way to do this is called indoor residual spraying, or IRS. Mosquitoes tend to rest on walls after taking a blood meal. IRS is a method of controlling mosquitoes indoors by coating the walls and other indoor surfaces with an insecticide. The insecticide kills the mosquitoes after they have fed, before they can bite another person. IRS programs were used frequently in the late 1950s and 1960s but were reduced because of the cost and concerns over the impact of the insecticides used. With the introduction of safer chemicals and the success of newer IRS programs, interest in IRS has started to return.

Another focus of insect control deals with reducing the number of mosquito larvae in an area. Mosquitoes breed in small patches of standing water such as ponds, puddles, rain barrels, and ditches. This is a challenge because many of these patches of water appear after a rain and then disappear, so it can be difficult to find and eliminate them in time to prevent the larvae from maturing. Areas of standing water that cannot be eliminated can be sprayed with insecticides or oils to kill the larvae.

A third area of research targeting mosquitoes involves genetically engineering malaria-resistant mosquitoes. Researchers at the University of Arizona have developed a genetically modified mosquito in which the malaria parasite cannot develop. The modification also shortens the mosquito's life span. The hope is that this mosquito will be able to breed with malaria-carrying mosquitoes so that the parasite cannot be carried to humans. "They have tested it on the most harmful of the malaria parasites, *Plasmodium falciparum*," says Gareth Lycett, a malaria researcher. "It is another step on the journey towards potentially assisting malaria control through GM [genetically modified] mosquito release."[22]

The fight against malaria has been a long and difficult one, but stepped-up efforts in the past ten years have made a difference. The CDC estimates that since 2001, as many as 3.3 million lives have been saved, and the death rate has been cut by 45 percent, fueling optimism that this deadly disease may someday be eradicated from the earth.

Fighting Waterborne Parasites

Clean, safe water is essential for human life, but according to WHO, approximately 3.4 million people worldwide, most of them children, die from waterborne illnesses each year. According to a report issued by the United Nations, four out of every ten people in the world do not have clean water for drinking, bathing, or cooking. "At any given time," says Erik Peterson of the Center for Strategic and International Studies in Washington, D.C.,

> close to half the population of the developing world is suffering from waterborne diseases associated with inadequate provision of water and sanitation services. There are about four billion cases of diarrhea disease per year, result-

Nearly half the population of the developing world is suffering from waterborne diseases associated with a lack of clean water.

ing in about one or two million deaths, some ninety percent of which, tragically, are in children under the age of five.[23]

Many of the most devastating parasitic infections, including ascariasis, schistosomiasis, amoebic dysentery, and giardiasis, are transmitted through contact with contaminated water. Health organizations such as the CDC and WHO, along with other national and international health agencies and national governments, are involved in many parts of the world to help provide clean water. For example, the CDC's global WASH (water, sanitation, hygiene) program provides knowledge, research, and interventions aimed at reducing waterborne parasitic diseases. The WASH program focuses on six specific areas: collecting data on the causes of these diseases; making available water safe; improving hygiene and sanitation measures in communities; responding to emergencies that affect water supply, such as disease outbreaks, wars, and natural disasters; controlling and eliminating waterborne NTDs; and providing education to people about sanitation and hygiene.

Controlling Vector-Borne Diseases

Controlling and preventing illnesses caused by arthropod vectors such as fleas, flies, ticks, and mites is probably the biggest challenge of all. These are extremely successful organisms that have existed on the planet for about 400 million years and have been closely involved with humans for thousands of years. According to the CDC, "Vector-borne diseases are especially difficult to predict, prevent or control. Only a few have vaccines. Mosquitoes and ticks are notoriously difficult to reach and often develop resistance to insecticides. Adding to the complexity, almost all vector-borne pathogens are zoonoses, meaning they can live in animals as well as in humans."[24]

Increasing global travel, changing land-use patterns, and global climate change have all contributed to changing patterns in many vector-borne diseases over the past several decades. First, as people travel and migrate around the world, they carry arthropod vectors with them, as well as the organisms carried by the vectors. Chagas' disease, which is increasing in the United States due partly to increased immigration from Central and South America, is an example of this. Second, with a rapidly increasing world population, more land is being converted to agricultural use, which greatly affects natural insect habitat and behavior. More animals being used for meat consumption provide more intermediate hosts for all kinds of ectoparasites. Collections of water for irrigating crops create fertile breeding areas for mosquitoes. Third, because insects are extremely susceptible to changes in climate, rapidly increasing global temperatures beginning in the last half of the twentieth century have made it possible for insects to live longer, breed more often, and live in larger geographic areas.

Reducing vector-borne illnesses, therefore, cannot rely on completely eliminating vectors from the environment. Research on controlling these diseases focuses on several major areas. First, because most of these illnesses occur in underdeveloped areas of the world, it is important to gather as much information as possible about where they occur and how their geographic distribution is changing, so that control efforts can be directed to the areas that need it most. Second, new diagnostic testing methods are needed that are fast, accurate, easy to administer, and affordable, so that new cases can be caught

A health worker in Africa sprays an insecticide to eradicate disease-carrying mosquitoes.

Mass Drug Administration

Mass drug administration (MDA) is the practice of giving a cura-tive dose of a drug to an entire population of people, regardless of whether they actually have the disease or not, in an effort to stop its spread. Six of WHO's NTDs (five of the six are parasitic diseases) are considered controllable through MDA. MDA has been used in malaria-endemic areas since the early 1930s, but overuse of the technique was believed to have created resistance to the drugs used. As a result, it is currently used only when there is an outbreak in a particular area, such as a town or village, or for specific populations of people such as pregnant women, infants, and school-age children.

In 1997 the World Health Assembly passed a resolution calling for the elimination of lymphatic filariasis by 2020, and MDA is part of that effort in many countries in which lymphatic filariasis is widespread. Usually, these programs consist of distribution of drugs to the entire population of endemic areas once a year for five years. The goal is for at least 80 percent of the people in the area to get the drugs. The cost of these programs is relatively low; they are supported by donations from drug companies, govern-ment agencies, and private corporations. One area of success is American Samoa, an island nation in the Pacific, in which MDA began in 2000 and resulted in a sharp decline in cases of lym-phatic filariasis (from 11.5 percent to less than 1 percent) after the five-year period.

early. Third, a great deal of study is taking place into new drugs that are also effective, inexpensive, and easy to administer. Education is also an important way to help control the occur-rence and spread of vector-borne diseases. Health-care work-ers around the world devote a great deal of time to educating people in endemic areas about how to prevent contact with insect vectors, how to recognize early symptoms of disease, and what to do if symptoms arise.

Parasites and parasitic diseases of all kinds will most likely always be a part of human life, and fighting against them is a constant struggle. The world's human population is growing more rapidly than at any time in history, providing a constantly increasing supply of susceptible human hosts for parasites. Great strides have been made, however, in reducing the incidence of these diseases and minimizing their impact on human health and quality of life. NTDs are finally gaining the scientific and financial attention they deserve, and some, such as guinea worm disease, are close to being eradicated once and for all.

Notes

Introduction: Unwelcome Guests

1. F.E.G. Cox. "History of Human Parasitology." *Clinical Microbiology Reviews,* October 2002, p. 595. http://cmr.asm.org/content/15/4/595.full.
2. Quoted in David Grove. *Tapeworms, Lice, and Prions: A Compendium of Unpleasant Infections.* Oxford: Oxford University Press, 2014, p. 116.
3. Carl Zimmer. "Do Parasites Rule the World?" *Discover,* August 1, 2000. http://discovermagazine.com/2000/aug/cover.
4. Quoted in Centers for Disease Control and Prevention. "Parasitic Infections Also Occur in the United States," May 8, 2014. www.cdc.gov/media/releases/2014/p0508-npi.html.
5. Quoted in ScienceDaily. "Urban Sprawl Promotes Worm Exchange Across Species," January 28, 2015. www.sciencedaily.com/releases/2015/01/150128093435.htm.

Chapter One: What Are Parasites?

6. Zimmer. "Do Parasites Rule the World?"
7. About Bioscience. "Bioscience Careers." North Carolina Association for Biomedical Research. www.aboutbioscience.org/careers/parasitologist.

Chapter Two: Protozoans

8. Quoted in Thomasine E. Lewis Tilden. *Belly-Busting Worm Invasions! Parasites That Love Your Insides!* New York: Scholastic, 2007, p. 38.
9. Quoted in MedicineNet. "Patient Comments—Toxoplasmosis Symptoms," August 5, 2014. www.medicinenet.com/toxoplasmosis/patient-comments-773.htm.

Chapter Three: Malaria

10. Quoted in *World Heritage Encyclopedia*. "Patrick Manson," 2014. www.worldheritage.org/articles/Patrick_Manson.
11. Ann Paisley Chandler. "Personal Story: Living Through Malaria." Malaria No More, June 28, 2011. www.malaria nomore.org/news/blog/personal-story-living-through -malaria.

Chapter Four: Helminths

12. Albert Marrin. *Little Monsters: The Creatures That Live on Us and in Us*. New York: Dutton, 2011, p. 111.
13. Quoted in ScienceDaily. "Availability and Use of Sanitation Reduces by Half the Likelihood of Parasitic Worm Infections," January 25, 2012. www.sciencedaily.com /releases/2012/01/120124184152.htm.

Chapter Five: Ectoparasites

14. Quoted in Alex Wild. "Giving Birth to a Tropical Parasite." Video. *Compound Eye* (blog), *Scientific American*, January 12, 2015. http://blogs.scientificamerican.com /compound-eye/2015/01/12/giving-birth-to-parasite.
15. Marrin. *Little Monsters*, p. 1.
16. Quoted in Anonymous. "I Have a Story About Lyme Disease." Video. Disease Detectives. www.diseasedetectives .org/stories/lyme.

Chapter Six: Parasitic Diseases Today and in the Future

17. Quoted in William E. Hoyle, trans. *The Parasites of Man, and the Diseases Which Proceed from Them: A Textbook for Students and Practitioners*. Author's preface to English edition, 1886, p. vii. www.todayinsci.com/L/Leuckart _Karl/LeuckartKarl-Quotations.htm.
18. Carlos M. Morel. "Neglected Diseases: Underfunded Research and Inadequate Health Interventions." *EMBO Reports*, June 2003. www.ncbi.nlm.nih.gov/pmc/articles /PMC1326440.

19. Centers for Disease Control and Prevention. "Neglected Tropical Diseases." www.cdc.gov/globalhealth/ntd.

20. Quoted in World Health Organization. "Single Repository to Bolster Storage and Exchange of NTD Data," November 24, 2014. www.who.int/neglected_diseases/ntd_data _single_repository/en.

21. Centers for Disease Control and Prevention. "Malaria." www.cdc.gov/malaria/index.html.

22. Quoted in Victoria Gill. "Malaria-Proof Mosquito Engineered." BBC News, July 16, 2010. www.bbc.co.uk/news /science-environment-10654599.

23. Quoted in Jessica Berman. "WHO: Water-Borne Disease Is World's Leading Killer." Voice of America, October 29, 2009. www.voanews.com/content/a-13-2005-03-17-voa 34-67381152/274768.html.

24. Centers for Disease Control and Prevention. "About the Division of Vector-Borne Diseases." www.cdc.gov/ncezid /dvbd/about.html.

Glossary

definitive host: The host organism in which the parasite lives during its most active stages of growth and reproduction.

ectoparasite: A parasite that lives on the outside of its host, in or on the skin.

endoparasite: A parasite that lives inside the body cavities or organs of its hosts.

eukaryotic: A cell that has a defined nucleus that contains its genetic material.

facultative parasite: A parasite that can live without a host for part of its life.

hermaphrodite: An animal whose body has both male and female reproductive organs.

host: Any organism on which a parasite lives and from which it takes what it needs for survival.

intermediate host: The host organism in which the parasite lives for part of its life before becoming infective.

metamorphosis: The process through which an insect changes from its larval stage to its adult stage while inside a pupa or chrysalis.

obligate parasite: A parasite that must spend its entire life in a host organism in order to survive.

parasite: An organism that lives and feeds on another organism and harms it in some way.

pathogen: An organism that causes disease in another organism.

protists: The kingdom of simple eukaryotic organisms that includes protozoans, algae, and slime molds.

symbiotic: Any relationship between organisms of different species that live together and interact in some way.

vector: An organism, usually an insect, that carries a parasite or other pathogen and transmits it to another organism.

zoonosis: A disease that can be transmitted to humans from another animal, such as toxoplasmosis or swine flu.

Organizations to Contact

Centers for Disease Control and Prevention (CDC)

1600 Clifton Rd.
Atlanta, GA 30329-4027
(800) 232-4636
www.cdc.gov

The CDC is part of the U.S. Department of Health and Human Services. It works in the United States and around the world to help protect Americans from threats to their health and safety from any cause and from any part of the world. They also provide extensive education on health and safety issues for the public as well as for policy makers in the government.

National Institutes of Health (NIH)

9000 Rockville Pike
Bethesda, MD 20892
(301) 496-4000
http://nih.gov

Like the CDC, the NIH is part of the U.S. Department of Health and Human Services. The NIH focuses its efforts on funding, conducting, and supporting medical research in many areas of human health and wellness.

Water.org

920 Main St., Ste. 1800
Kansas City, MO 64105
(816) 877-8400
http://water.org

Water.org is a nonprofit organization that helps provide safe drinking water and effective sanitation to people in Africa, Asia, and Central America.

World Health Organization (WHO)

Avenue Appia 20
1211 Geneva 27, Switzerland
+ 41 22 791 21 11
www.who.int/en

WHO is the United Nations' coordinating body for world health issues. It helps shape health-related government policies and research agendas, sets standards for health-care and living conditions, monitors worldwide health trends, and provides support for nations in their health-related efforts.

For More Information

Books

Paul Fleischer. *Parasites: Latching On to a Free Lunch*. New York: Century, 2006. An easy-to-read illustrated book about all kinds of parasites of plants, animals, and humans.

Kris Hirschmann. *Lice*. San Diego, CA: Kidhaven, 2004. Provides a brief overview of lice, describing what they are, how they affect people and animals, and how to avoid getting lice.

Thomasine E. Lewis Tilden. *Belly-Busting Worm Invasions! Parasites That Love Your Insides!* New York: Franklin Watts, 2008. A book about parasites that includes stories of real people with parasitic worm illnesses.

Albert Marrin. *Little Monsters: The Creatures That Live On Us and In Us*. New York: Dutton, 2011. Describes parasites that live on or in the human body, including mosquitoes, head lice, mites, fleas, and worms. Includes interesting historical accounts about parasites.

Jennifer Viegas. *Parasites*. New York: Rosen, 2004. Explains what parasites are, describes the three basic parasite groups, discusses the human diseases and disorders that can be caused by parasites, and looks at ways to prevent or treat infestations.

Websites

Malaria No More (www.malarianomore.org). A group dedicated to ending malaria by engaging world leaders, raising public awareness and education, and delivering life-saving tools and education throughout Africa.

Malaria Site (www.malariasite.com/index.htm). A comprehensive site featuring information on the history of malaria, the parasite itself, and clinical features, diagnosis, treatment, complications, and control of malaria.

Medline Plus (www.nlm.nih.gov/medlineplus). The National Institutes of Health's website for patients, families, and friends. Produced by the National Library of Medicine, it provides up-to-date health information about all kinds of diseases, conditions, and wellness issues in easy-to-understand language.

PARA-SITE (http://parasite.org.au/para-site/introduction). An educational site from the Australian Society of Parasitology. Offers general information about parasites that cause disease in both animals and people.

Parasites in Humans (www.parasitesinhumans.org). An informative website about parasitic infections caused by worms, microscopic protozoans, and skin parasites, with links to pages about specific parasites and the diseases they cause.

Parasitology.com (http://parasitology.com). A comprehensive site with information about parasites, parasitic diseases, and news articles about parasites.

World of Parasites (www3.sympatico.ca/james.smith090/WORLDOF.HTM). An interactive world map in which the reader can click on a country to see which parasites occur there.

Index

Picture Credits

Cover: © Schubbell/Shutterstock.com

© Alan & Linda Detrick/Science Source, 19

© Alan Carey/Science Source, 41

© Andy Crump, TDR, World Health Organization/Science Source, 37, 55, 109

© AP Images/John Bazemore, 101

© AP Images/Kyodo, 77

© Biophoto Associates/Science Source, 22

© Everett Collection Historical/Alamy, 9

© Everett Collection, Inc./Alamy, 58

© Eye of Science/Science Source, 13, 20, 66

© Francis Leroy/Science Source, 30

© Gale/Cengage Learning, 53, 62

© John Greim/Science Source, 99

© Julie Dermansky/Science Source, 107

© London School of Hygiene & Tropical medicine/Science Source, 33

© Patti McConville/Alamy, 57

© Phillipe Psalia/Science Source, 85

© R. Unmesh Chandran, TDR, WHO/Science Source, 73

© Science Picture Co/Science Source, 61, 71, 88

© Science Source, 47, 50, 91

© Springer Medzin/Science Sourcc, 67

© St. Bartholomew's Hospital/Science Source, 87

© Steen Drozd Lund/Science Source, 81

© Ted Kinsman/Science Source, 15

© Vaughan Fleming/Science Source, 94

© VEM/Science Source, 34

© Zeijko Vala/Alamy, 25

About the Author

Lizabeth Craig received her bachelor of science in nursing from the University of Florida and her bachelor of science in secondary education from Southwest Missouri State University. She began writing as a serious hobby in 2003 and has since published both fiction and nonfiction for kids and adults. She lives in Spring Hill, Florida, where she works as a surgical nurse and takes care of her husband, Richard, two dogs, one cat, a coop of chickens, and a vegetable garden. *Parasitic Diseases* is her fourteenth book for Lucent Books.